ARMANDO TOCCI

COPYRIGHT INFORMATION

Text copyright © Armando Tocci Publishing House 2023 All rights reserved.

The right of Armando Tocci to be identified as the author of this work has been asserted by him in accordance with The Commonwealth Copyright Act 1968.

No part of this publication may be reproduced, distributed, or transmitted in any form or by any means, including photocopying, recording, or other electronic or mechanical methods, without the prior written permission of the publisher, except in the case of brief quotations embodied in reviews and certain other non-commercial uses permitted by copyright law.

ISBN: 978-0-6458507-0-3

Original Photo by Vaynakh on Freepik.com
Adobe Fonts Library and Google Fonts used and are cleared for both personal and commercial use under the Open Font License.

Scripture quotations
New King James Version (NKJV)
New International Version (NIV)
New Living Translation (NLT)
New American Standard Bible (NASB)
English Standard Version (ESV)
The Message (MSG)

The Armor of God

'Finally, be strong in the Lord and in his mighty power. Put on the full armor of God, so that you can take your stand against the devil's schemes. For our struggle is not against flesh and blood, but against the rulers, against the authorities, against the powers of this dark world and against the spiritual forces of evil in the heavenly realms. Therefore put on the full armor of God, so that when the day of evil comes, you may be able to stand your ground, and after you have done everything, to stand. Stand firm then, with the belt of truth buckled around your waist, with the breastplate of righteousness in place, and with your feet fitted with the readiness that comes from the gospel of peace. In addition to all this, take up the shield of faith, with which you can extinguish all the flaming arrows of the evil one. Take the helmet of salvation and the sword of the Spirit, which is the word of God.'

Ephesians 6:10-18 NIV

CONTENTS

	Acknowledgements	7
	Preface	11
One	The Second Man	13
Two	Born to be Wild	29
Three	The Journey	47
Four	The Choice is Yours	59
Five	The Fight	69
Six	Understanding the Battlefield	79
Seven	Entering the New El Dorado	97
Eight	The Call	115
Nine	A New Life	133
Ten	A Broken Heart (Part One)	147
Eleven	A Broken Heart (Part Two)	159
Twelve	Healing & Redemption	171
Thirteen	The Invisible Chapter	199
	References	203

ACKNOWLEDGEMENTS

Dear God, I am filled with deep gratitude as I reflect on the completion of my book. It is with a heart brimming with thankfulness that I acknowledge the guidance, inspiration, and strength You have bestowed upon me throughout this creative journey. In moments of uncertainty, You provided clarity and purpose, nurturing the seed of creativity within me. Your divine wisdom illuminated my path, allowing my words to flow and take shape on the pages. With every chapter, I felt Your presence gently nudging me forward and unveiling new ideas. I am grateful for the opportunities to touch hearts, inspire minds, and make a positive impact through the written word. This book is a testament to Your grace, as You allowed me to be a vessel for your message. Thank You, God, for instilling within me the courage and perseverance to bring this book into existence. Without Your unwavering support and love, this accomplishment would not have been possible. May this work be a testament to Your glory and a source of inspiration and comfort for those who read it.

To all my family members and friends that have supported me in this long-term project, I extend my heartfelt thanks.

I would like to take a moment to express my deepest gratitude to my wife Isabella for her unwavering support throughout the entire process of writing this book. Through the toughest of times and despite my self-doubt, her love, patience, and encouragement have been the backbone of my journey, and I could not have done it without her. Her understanding and empathy have been a constant source of motivation, even during the toughest of times. I am truly blessed to have her in my life. Thank you, my love, for being my rock, my inspiration, and my greatest supporter. I could not have done this without you, and I am forever grateful for your steadfast love and support.

I would like to extend a sincere thank you to my good friend Andrew Drummond for his support and guidance throughout the process of writing this book. His encouragement and insights have been instrumental in making this journey a success. Andrew's experience as an author, and his keen eye for detail have been invaluable. His willingness to share his wisdom and to provide constructive feedback has helped me to refine my work and to bring my vision to life. More than that, Andrew has been a true friend, always there with a listening ear and a kind word of encouragement when I need it most. His generosity of spirit has been a constant source of motivation and inspiration. Thank you, Andrew, for all that you have done for me. Your guidance, friendship, and support have meant the world to me, and I will always be grateful for your persistent belief in me and my work.

I wanted to also thank my editor and graphic designer, Renee Ges, by taking a moment to express my gratitude for all the hard work and dedication she has put into editing my book. Your keen eye for detail and your insightful suggestions have helped to shape my manuscript into something truly remarkable. Your professionalism and commitment to excellence have not gone unnoticed, and I am so grateful to have had the opportunity to work with you. Thank you for all the time and effort you invested in this project.

PREFACE

My desire to write a book arose in my twenties. Back then I didn't really know what to write about. As years passed, I understood that the best thing I could do to start writing a book was to write about my experiences, the things I had learned, and to share with people my life lessons and failures. In this book, I share my life story and journey to discovering God's call on my life, despite all the struggles and difficulties I faced. I learned many lessons along the way that I wouldn't have learned otherwise. I will be speaking about the constant internal fight we have between our old self, which I call the second man, and our new self after conversion.

The Bible is full of examples of people that have been called to serve God: Joseph, Joshua, Peter, Paul, and many others. In the present-day world, we are called to do God's work too.

It does not matter if we are called for a specific ministry or a more generic task. 1 Corinthians 10:31 states that whatever work we do, to 'do it all for the glory of God'.

If God gives you a task, accept it cheerfully and do it with diligence. If God has not given you a specific call or assignment, then seek to fulfil the common mission for all believers: to love, obey, and serve God.

chapter one
THE SECOND MAN

While reading the title of this book you may be asking yourself, 'Who is this second man? What is this guy talking about?' Allow me to explain. The second man is the one who can ruin God's plan for you. Many Christians today commit the mistake of blaming the devil for their failures and mistakes, when in fact they have allowed the second man to take over their spiritual lives.

During my life journey, I have learned that the most significant and vital question to answer in ministry is not about leadership styles, techniques or know how. It is about understanding who can destroy God's plan for your life and how they would accomplish that. If we can understand this principle, then our chances of success and longevity in ministry has intensely increased. Many writers have produced books on leadership, giving various suggestions and ideas on the topic. However, do they essentially and straightforwardly answer the single most important question on the subject?

Churches have an indispensable obligation for leadership for the purpose of growing and becoming more productive. However, there are certain questions that must be asked such as, 'What are the most important yet the most difficult things to do in ministry?' and, 'What is to be said for the man who is called to ministry?' It begins with comprehending what ministry truly is.

On one occasion, Jesus made it very clear what ministry is all about. The apostle John writes about when Jesus appeared to his disciples for the third time after his resurrection.

> 'Jesus said to Simon Peter, "Simon son of John, do you love me more than these?" "Yes, Lord," he said, "you know that I love you." Jesus said, "Feed my lambs." Again Jesus said, "Simon son of John, do you love me?" He answered, "Yes, Lord, you know that I love you."

> Jesus said, "Take care of my sheep."'
>
> *John 21:15-17 NIV*

In other words, Jesus is telling Peter to look after people. Whatever form that might take, the core objective remains that ministry is entirely about people.

Serving God by looking after His people is certainly not an easy task, it takes courage and sacrifice. The reality is that there isn't much teaching in Bible colleges today regarding how to deal with your second man, whilst being involved in ministry. In my experience there was no real conversation about the personal struggles that you must inevitably face. Ministry is not just a task, it is a lifestyle that we adopt and live out until the very end, with no compromises.

Another truth that we should not forget is the fact that God is using human beings to accomplish His work. God's love is unconditional. He accepts us just the way we are. He knows that we are not perfect, and He still calls us to serve. We must remember that despite God's grace, we need to play our part. Many people have the misconception that being in ministry is all about glamour and success. It is notably hard work, and much sacrifice is required to make it function and thrive.

We need to understand what endangers God's plan in our life so we can avoid it. More than ever, we need to be aware of what can stop us from being victorious in life, and instead advance in all that God has planned for us. The Bible makes it clear that it is imperative to be watchful over the second man.

Why do some people desire to know God and the Bible while others seem to do all they can to avoid it? I have asked myself this question. Paul tells us that there are two types of people in this world: the second man and the spiritual man.

The Second Man
What is the second man? The word second refers to that which is given to the lusts and desires of the flesh. Rather than living to please God, the second man lives to please self. Paul describes many of the actions of the second man in Galatians 5:19-21 NLT.

> 'When you follow the desires of your sinful nature, the results are very clear: sexual immorality, impurity, lustful pleasures, idolatry, sorcery, hostility, quarrelling, jealousy, outbursts of anger, selfish ambition, dissension, division, envy, drunkenness, wild parties, and other sins like these. Let me tell you again, as I have before, that anyone living that sort of life will not inherit the Kingdom of God.'

So often we hear in the news of people committing revolting crimes and we wonder why. They do so because they are spiritually dead. God's presence and influence are absent from their life. Therefore, they are left to focus only upon what will gratify their fleshly desires. The biblical term for their condition is godless. The word godless means just what it says: God-less. In addition to this, Paul tells us other important truths about the second man. First, we see that he is unreceptive to the things of God. Rather than accepting God's spiritual truths, the second man rejects them and sometimes even resents them. Due to his unregenerate nature, it causes him to be antagonistic towards God and His Word. He views salvation and surrender to Christ as foolishness and a waste of time. 'Why live for God when you can live for yourself?' is his philosophy of life. The Bible cites that the way of the second man is like grass, '"their beauty is like a flower in the field. The grass withers and the flower fades"' (1 Peter 1:24 NLT, Isaiah 40:6-8 NIV).

The Spiritual Man

When someone appeals to God and seeks forgiveness in Jesus his sins are removed, he is cleansed, his relationship with God is restored, and he is transformed into a 'new creation: The old has gone, the new is here!' (2 Corinthians 5:17 NIV). The second man is gone, and the new spiritual man is born. In John 1:12-13 NLT, we read that the new spiritual man is a newborn, brought about by the will of God. In other words, the new nature is a gift which we ought to cultivate. The new creation has his eyes now focused solely on Jesus instead of on worldly things as it once was.

Salvation has always been and will always be the plan

for mankind. The born-again experience makes everything new. The old is gone, and now there is a lot of space for the new to come in and develop and mature. The new spiritual man starts to see things differently. He realises that he has a purpose in life and that God has laid down a perfect plan in front of him. The Word of God becomes his compass and nourishing food for his spirit. The Bible describes this as putting 'off the old man with his deeds' (see Colossians 3:9-10 NKJV), and putting on the 'new self, created to be like God in true righteousness and holiness' (Ephesians 4:24 NIV).

What constitutes the new man is a spiritual mind, or a disposition to please God instead of self. The mind is fully committed to pleasing God, so that this becomes the chief end for which the individual lives and acts. The new man is thoroughly committed to do the will of God, just as the second man is committed to do the commands of his fleshly impulses. Besides these two ultimate ends, no other can be considered. These two dispositions divide all mankind into two classes. The Bible represents all men as either saints or sinners, holy or unholy, spiritual or natural. We can choose to either serve God or the devil, we cannot serve both at the same time. It makes them either old men or new men, born of the flesh or born of the Spirit. The new man is born of the Spirit, born from above. The Spirit of God continually affects his moral activity, leading him to thoroughly renounce self, and commit his whole being to do what God says. The new man surrenders totally to God. Then we start to become like Christ, His very Spirit now governing in our hearts and leading us through the stages of life. This does not happen from one day to the next, it is a constant process that occurs in our life as we continue putting on our new man.

This act of putting off the second man and putting on the new is precisely what the Bible means by regeneration. It is a constant ongoing action which transforms our entire life in every respect. This is the change of heart of which the Bible speaks. Selfishness is put away and Christ is put on in all things. This is the very essence of the Apostle's meaning. Putting off the second man and putting on the new man requires entire consecration to God. It means renouncing the dominion of the flesh and submitting to the dominion of the Spirit. Therefore,

John the Baptist said '"He must become greater; I must become less"' (John 3:30 NIV).

Our goal is to walk daily with Jesus, to become like him with our words and in our actions, to let Him consume us so that all of what we are fades away, until all of what He is can be seen. This constant death of the second man is, in my opinion one of, if not the most difficult thing to do in this process. The second man wants to rise every day and run his own show, wanting to gain back control of everything. He wants to lead, not to be led. The predominant change that needs to occur in our lives when putting on the new man is to understand that the things from our past are no longer our masters. In fact, we have no master but God. An extremely important ingredient needed for progression is perseverance. Perseverance is a steady persistence in a course of action or a purpose. It presses on despite difficulties, obstacles, or discouragement. Paul is writing to Christians and urges them to put off the second man with his deeds and put on the new man. He must mean that they should steadily maintain the activities they began to do at their conversion. This will only be possible if we persevere in changing our mindset.

During this transformation from old to new we get given a new divine mindset. The things of God have now become our main resource. Our focus and mindset are in tune with heavenly things. The things from above are now what we desire most. Our mindset has shifted its focus from the earthly things to heavenly things. All the earthly things have now become secondary. It is here where the new man directs his heart to long for the things above. This is the reason why the Bible says to 'store up for yourselves treasures in heaven, where neither moth nor rust destroys, and where thieves do not break in or steal; for where your treasure is, there your heart will be also' (Matthew 6:20-21 NASB). By securing treasure in heaven, we place ourselves in living connection with God who owns all the treasures of the earth and supplies all temporal mercies that are essential for life.

Considering everything that has been said so far, it is important once again to highlight the fact that this process is a lifelong exercise. Sometimes we will manage to succeed and sometimes we will fail. Nevertheless, the significant point is to never give up. Realise that the second man is in fact who we are at birth and who we will continue to be until we meet Christ. The second man is only the beginning of self and not the end. However, he is always present and tries to conduct our life in the way that he wants. Now as we embrace God's salvation and His marvelous plan for our life, our second man enters into battle since he is not in tune with the things of God. He does not understand the things from above. His sinful nature limits his access to God. His first appearance goes as far back as Adam and Eve. Since then, he has made it difficult for mankind to be what it should have been in the first place. Thank God that He sent His son Jesus to re-establish order and to offer a way back into God's mighty plan.

God is good and His desire is to see us flourish in life, to see us grow and live the dream. Keep in mind that in many things, the second man and the new man externally behave alike. They both eat and drink, and both use the necessities of life, but with one broad, fundamental distinction — one has no other end than self-gratification while the other lives for the glory of God. One aims only to please himself, the other only to please God. Their motives and ultimate end are just as different now as they will be when one of them shall be in heaven and the other in hell. Therefore, it is so important to kill the second man, leaving him no chance to destroy everything that you have ever hoped for. If we do not kill him, he will lead you away from God's plan, always interfering with God's purpose for our life.

The Bible recounts many examples of Godly men who gave space to the second man and failed in their determination for God. One of those men is Samson. Most of us are familiar with the life of Samson. If you grew up attending Sunday school, you probably heard many stories of his great strength and accomplishments. He was, without a doubt, the strongest man to ever walk the earth, and at the same time he was also one of the weakest. Personally, I think that the story of Samson is one of the saddest stories in the Bible. Here was a man with tremendous potential. He had godly parents, supernatural strength, and the Lord's favour. He literally had more gifts and more advantages than anyone else in his era. He was born, called, and used by God to serve as a living picture of divine deliverance. His birth was supernatural, and he suffered for the sake of his people. Everything about him was amazing, except for the fact that he never managed to control the second man in him. Scripture records several deeds of spiritual failure in his life. He was especially inclined to the kind of fleshly failure that is driven from uncontrolled lust, mixed with a lack of personal discipline. In other words, he could not control his fleshly desires. Obviously, the story of Samson is a familiar one and often used to teach us a very simple principle in ministry — to let your ministry be led by the spiritual man and not the second man.

Growing up as a Christian, I questioned the reasons for Samson's failure. By studying his story, I learned that it came down to the things I mentioned earlier. Instead of nourishing the spiritual man in him, he gave self-rule to his second man. This led him to eventually ignore spiritual values. His mind and heart had begun to drift away from God. His focus had shifted and became carnal, not spiritual. The bigger consequence was that he ignored God's plan, with the outcome being that he never became the deliverer that God had intended for him to become. The second man will keep us from becoming the godly leader that God wants us to become.

> God, help us to not become like Samson
> and waste the potential and purpose
> that You have given us.

Unfortunately, I have met many people who are modern day Samsons, folks with so much potential for being used of God, but for one reason or another they have wasted their lives. Despite of what we may think about the life of Samson, he is not only mentioned in the Bible to show us his failures, but more so for us to understand that most men who made history also failed at some point. Some of these men drastically failed, yet others refused to stay lying down in the dust. Their failure and repentance secured for them a greater understanding of the grace of God. Let's not forget that Samson appears in the heroes list among the great heroes of faith in Hebrews 11:32-34. That is a significant point to note because it presents Samson as a hero, not because of what he did or because of his supernatural strength, but because of his faith.

It is interesting to note that Scripture never tries to whitewash the heroes of the faith. Scripture paints these men realistically, even when the truth about them is negative. Samson was a man of great physical strength, but with a great moral weakness. When we read in Scripture about his moral failures, the lesson we're supposed to draw from it is not primarily a lesson about human failures but a great example of how God works through His grace, even when we have completely messed it up. In other words, the Bible never refrains from telling us about the failures of our spiritual ancestors. What Scripture aims to highlight is the grace of God, not the piety of people. If we lose sight of that distinction, we'll miss the whole point of the gospel. It's about the righteousness of Christ, provided by grace through faith for sinners who have no real righteousness of their own. Jesus stated, 'those who are well have no need of a physician, but those who are sick' (Luke 5:31 NKJV).

Samson was a redeemed man, but he continually got entangled by his second man who caused him to repeatedly sin and stumble. He continued associating with fleshly activities that he really ought to have put to death. Ultimately, those sins cost him his eyesight, his freedom, and finally his life. The reality is that we need to habitually kill the second man, or he will kill us. Samson's life is a perfect illustration of this principle. The way a leader confronts his own failure will have a significant effect on his future ministry.

chapter two
BORN TO BE WILD

'For you created my inmost being; you knit me together in my mother's womb. I praise you because I am fearfully and wonderfully made; your works are wonderful, I know that full well. My frame was not hidden from you when I was made in the secret place, when I was woven together in the depths of the earth. Your eyes saw my unformed body; all the days ordained for me were written in your book before one of them came to be.'

Psalm 139:13–16 NIV

God knew you long before you were born or even conceived. He thought about you and planned for you. When you feel discouraged or inadequate, remember that God has always valued you, and He has a purpose in mind for you. I'm sure that at some point in life we've all asked, 'What's my purpose? Am I called to something specific? What do I need to do?'

I started to be challenged with these types of questions at the young age of thirteen or fourteen years old. I recall sitting on a park bench one day after a soccer match, dreaming about the future, wondering what my future could look like. I saw myself playing soccer for big teams, experiencing the rush from being applauded and cheered on by large crowds. Even though I was just a kid at the time, something in me was telling me that there was more to life. Something in me was burning but I didn't know what it was or why. You would think a teenager would have different thoughts running through his mind, yet here was a thirteen-year-old boy who was trying to find answers much bigger than himself. At the time, I didn't really understand what was going on in my mind. Through my life, I have wrestled many times with these intricate thoughts. I have learned that searching for those answers is a very normal thing to do, purely because God has planted that desire of knowledge in furtherance of leading us closer towards His master plan for our lives. He valued us before anyone else knew we would exist. He cared for us while we were in our mother's womb. He planned our life even before our body was being formed inside of our mother's womb. He values us higher than we value ourselves.

I learned to overcome all sorts of fears and to familiarise myself with the knowledge that God has a plan mapped out for my life. His plan will carry me throughout all the various stages in my life, a plan which goes far beyond my imagination. Even if I was not able to understand it all then, and I had unanswered questions, I knew deep down that God had it all under control.

God has a purpose for each one of us, we are all called to a specific purpose. Some roles seem more prominent than others, though in God's eyes, there is no difference between one and the other. One thing that is indisputable in both cases is the fact that for the plan of God to work in our lives, we need to constantly kill the second man.

It was on the 268th day of the year in 1976 when a freshly married young girl named Lucia had to be rushed to the hospital in the early hours of the morning. On this cold Saturday morning of September 25th, something new was about to happen. There she was, in pain and without her husband Roberto near her due to work commitments. What seemed a disheartening situation was soon to be the beginning of a new chapter in the life of this freshly established family. God was at work carrying out His plan. Meanwhile, Lucia's father-in-law had to quickly find someone that would drive them to the nearest hospital which was 33km away. The road to the hospital was a very dangerous mountain road. Fast driving wasn't possible since it would put everyone at high risk. Finally, the father-in-law got his nephew to drive them to the hospital in the city of Cosenza. Young Lucia was on her own with her father and mother-in-law.

The forty-minute drive to the hospital was nerve-wracking. When they eventually got to the hospital, the doctor immediately took care of the young, soon-to-be mother. A few hours later, an amazing sound filled the corridors of the hospital. It was the sound of a special, healthy, and crying newborn baby. Now that she could hold him and embrace him in her loving arms, all the pain and worries of birthing disappeared, and was replaced by pure delight, amazement, and joy. He was named Armando, only to discover the origin and meaning of the name later, and that he would live up to its meaning: man of war.

This is obviously the story of the beginning of my life. A few days later, mum and baby were released from the hospital and sent home, which was in a little town called Falconara Albanese, in the province of Cosenza, in the Calabrian region of southern Italy. Falconara is the only Albanian community located on the Tyrrhenian Sea. The site was populated in the early 1500s by people who were fleeing the threat of a Turkish invasion. These Albanians settled in this territory, bringing with them customs and traditions which are still practiced to this day. In 1976 the population was slightly over 5,000 inhabitants, including Roberto and his growing family. Viewing my family's life event as simple and ordinary would be a mistake. There's so much more to our story than the typical events that happen in ones' life, it's the execution of God's will and plan for this specific family as a collective, and every individual.

Before we can go any further, it is vital to understand and acknowledge that God has a plan for you. We don't need to go through life without any purpose. God has not created us so that we wander around without any aim. In John 10:10 Jesus stated, 'I came that they may have and enjoy life, and have it in abundance'. God's idea for us is to live our lives to the full. For this reason, He designs and proposes a master plan to us. Let's go through the various steps of this process to discover together important truths that will help us grasp God's plan for our lives. Jeremiah 1:5, God makes an interesting statement which gives us a clear insight on how He reasons. "Before I formed you in the womb I knew you, before you were born, I set you apart; I appointed you as a prophet to the nations" (Jeremiah 1:5 NIV). There are several wonderful and awe-inspiring points to find in this piece of text, as we reflect on what this verse says about the omniscience of God.

God tells Jeremiah that He 'knew' him before he was formed within the womb. He already knew Jeremiah's strengths and weaknesses. He also already knew that Jeremiah would possess what God wanted to use during this particularly trying time of Israel's history. Before Jeremiah was born, God had already set him aside for a special task which He later revealed to him as a young adult.

What does this mean to us? After all, we are not prophets like Jeremiah, but human beings created in God's image just like Jeremiah. God knows every one of us — our strengths and weaknesses, abilities, and limitations. He knew us in this way even before we were born.

One of the first things we need to understand as we discover God's plan for our lives is that it is up to us whether we will accept God's divine appointment or not, just as it was up to Jeremiah. Only through acceptance can God's plan unfold in our lives. Acknowledgment and acceptance are the first steps to take towards this marvellous plan that God has for us. Once we have made the decision to accept it, God will start to reveal its incredible truths.

The Bible teaches that God's design for mankind is found in His word. God has given us His Word so that we might find everything we need in the discovery of His will for our lives. In addition, we learn about who He is and how He functions. The Bible reveals God's good intentions and plans for us. It is through this marvellous gift that we can acknowledge His design for us. Jeremiah 29:11 NIV makes it very clear what God's intentions are.

> '"For I know the plans I have for you," declares the LORD, "plans to prosper you and not to harm you, plans to give you hope and a future"'.

God designed for our lives to have the very best of purpose, adventure, fulfilment, joy, and guidance under His righteous instruction. This does not mean that we will not face trials and tribulations. Despite all the beautiful promises of God for our lives, He has never declared that we won't encounter hardship. A profound promise that Jesus made is 'never will I leave you; never will I forsake you' (Hebrews 13:5, see also Joshua 1:5, Deuteronomy 31:6). No matter the circumstance we may find ourselves in, He will always be there for us. The apostle Paul understood that adversity would sometimes be part of our journey, and on many occasions in his letters and epistles we read about his suffering. Regardless, this is what Paul declares in Philippians 4:12-13 NIV.

> "'I know what it is to be in need, and I know what it is to have plenty. I have learned the secret of being content in any and every situation, whether well fed or hungry, whether living in plenty or in want. I can do all this through him who gives me strength.'"

Times of adversity came around very quickly for me. I was only 3 months old when doctors reported to my parents that I would die within the next 48 hours if no blood of the same type was found for a transfusion. What you need to know is that the blood type B negative is a rare blood type that holds tremendous power. Only 2% of the population has B negative blood. Back in 1976 this blood type was even rarer, and the doctors had given up hope. All parties involved were desperate in trying to find blood. All the major hospitals were being solicited with no results. Since no blood was available anywhere in the region, my only hope of survival was to find a donor with the same blood type. In other words, a miracle was needed. You see, even in the darkest hour of our life, God does not leave nor forsake us. Circumstances around us do not influence the rollout of God's plan in our life. What He has decided will stand.

Even if the circumstances around me were saying that I was going to die, God had other plans. God made a way where there was no way. Out of the blue an old lady that was living in a distant village came to see my parents at the hospital saying that she had heard about the search for this rare blood type. She explained that she remembered a doctor once telling her that she had a very rare blood type. After various examinations and cross-matching, it was determined that this lady was compatible as a donor as she also had the B negative blood type. The charitable woman agreed to a blood transfusion to save my life. What happened prior, causing this scary event to take place was that my blood had been poisoned. I was given powdered milk purchased from the village pharmacy. My parents unaware that it was past its expiry date. A very simple and routine act had turned into a nightmare. After an extended time in hospital, I started to recover and became healthy again. The testimony of the miracle spread fast, and everyone was amazed. I don't believe in coincidences, instead in the divine intervention of God's hand that has the power to create, change and restore.

God had a plan for my life, and He was not going to let that plan be ruined by this mishap. I learned that what seems unforeseen by us is not unforeseen by God. God is all-knowing and nothing can surprise Him. Growing up, my family and I had to go through many changes which have shaped, directed, and given flavour to my life. Initially I was very resistant towards these changes until one day God made me realise that all these changes were necessary for the fulfilment of His master plan in my life. Growing up in

Falconara Albanese till the age of eight was a great adventure. Living in this little village in the middle of the Calabrian Mountains, life was awesome — everybody knew each other, and a great sense of belonging dominated the atmosphere. As a child I was tempestuous and very lively. I always appeared as the leader of the village gang. I couldn't stand still for a minute. My mind was always busy thinking, 'What can we do next' and who can we tease afterwards?' I felt free and invincible. I used to dream with my eyes wide open, nothing was too hard or impossible. I viewed the world like a place that needed to be explored and conquered. This spontaneity was not always easy for my parents to manage, rather my constant cheekiness would create difficulties at school and in social environments. Even though I was considered the village mascot, enough was enough. I remember hearing my friends and teachers say, 'Who knows what this boy will become one day'.

A short time later, an unexpected event was about to take place that would change the course of my future and establish a new direction in my life. One day, as I arrived home from school, I saw my mum packing my dad's clothes in a suitcase. My initial thought was that we were going on vacation, although when I realized my mother's facial expression, I understood that it was not a joyous occasion. I asked my mum what was going on, and after much persistence, kneeling and with tears in her eyes, she explained to me that my father was going to Germany to find a new job. The news hit me like a punch in the face. For a few minutes I was speechless not knowing what had just transpired. Hundreds of questions bombarded my mind as my whole world collapsed. We had never spoken of this before nor were there any warning signs given. I was completely unprepared and totally incapable to accept the finality of this decision. I ran off in tears and full of anger, I could not understand why this was happening.

A six-year-old boy does not think about the financial situation of his family, let alone the socioeconomic status of his family. As a child you're unaware of these things and life just happens as per normal. Our family's financial situation was deteriorating quickly due to a lack of work for my father. The employment situation at that time in Italy was very unfortunate; many companies had declared bankruptcy, and as a result all the employees were made redundant. Many governments failed to guide the country well and were unable to get the economy in check causing inflation. In other words, our future in Italy was not looking bright.

Being confronted with this desperate reality, my father decided that the best thing to do was to leave Italy and look for a better life in a different country. At that time Germany was booming and developing quickly, and its industrial capacity was increasing fast. Many immigrants that were in the same situation had found an earnest hope in moving to Germany, it had become the new "El Dorado" of Europe. Germany had become one of the most important European destinations for foreigners. To play it safe my father decided to leave Italy alone at first, leaving behind my mother, myself, and my one-year-old brother Stefano. The idea was for him to go to Germany, find a permanent job and a place to live, then come back to Italy to then bring the rest of the family back with him once everything was in place. During that period, I remember being in complete denial and full of anger towards everyone and everything. I did not want to leave behind all my friends. In my village I was free, I felt like a king in his kingdom, unrestricted to do whatever pleased me, and I knew all this was about to change.

I had never heard about Germany before. I did not even know where it was geographically, let alone the fact that everything was different to what I was used to. My father returned a little over a year later for Christmas, bringing me and my brother many toys. For a while I had forgotten about my anger and discontent. Seeing Dad back home changed my world. It was early January of 1983, when my dad asked me to sit on his knee because he wanted to give me some good news. 'Son, in a few days I will need to go back to Germany, but I will be back soon to get you, Mum and your brother, and we will all be together again.' At that moment I didn't know what to say because I wasn't able to figure out what it meant. On this occasion, I remember my dad trying to explain to me that we would have a better life in Germany, a higher education, and an improved future for us all. At the time, I did not consider my father to be a hero for what he was doing, simply because I did not understand the impact and future benefits that this specific decision would eventually impart for us as a family, and for me as an individual.

Sometimes in our Christian walk, we can be a bit like this, angry and frustrated with God because He does not reveal His plan and purpose to us all at once. I have experienced on only a few occasions, where God decides to reveal his full plan at once. Assuredly, God's plan is unfolded and made visible to us as we walk in faith, putting our trust in Him alone. Let me say this my dear friends, allow God to be God and to direct your steps as He pleases.

Proverbs 20:24 NIV puts it this way, 'A person's steps are directed by the Lord. How then can anyone understand their own way?' Don't try to figure it all out before you have started. God knows exactly what he is doing, just let Him do what He needs to do. Let him reveal to you what He thinks is necessary for you at that specific moment. Don't try to push God and expect for Him to tell you everything, because He knows best. I can tell you that by doing things in your own strength that God will not answer, He will not respond. Proverbs 16:9 NIV 'In their hearts humans plan their course, but the LORD establishes their steps'. This passage has been so authentic for me and sometimes when I ponder on this, I wish I understood this verse much earlier, it would have saved me from much unnecessary lament.

Today I consider both of my parents as heroes for who they are and for what they did for me. They followed God's plan and purpose willingly and they sacrificed so much to give our family a better life. I think of how many people are truly prepared to sacrifice all they have for the purpose of living a better Christian life and developing and growing in both ministry and church life.

chapter three
THE JOURNEY

It was during a pleasant day in June of 1983, when my family and I travelled by train towards Germany. After one full year of my father being away, he had managed to find a permanent job and a place for us to live in a city called Mannheim. His promise to come back and get us had come to fruition. The eighteen-hour trip to a better life had begun. I remember too well the mixed emotions. On one hand, I was sad for having left behind extended family members and friends. On the other, I was excited to see what Germany would be like. So many thoughts were buzzing in my mind to the point that I couldn't think straight. As I stood on platform four at the train station waiting for our train to arrive, time stood still. Friends and family had come to farewell us, their sadness visible through attempted smiles. Looking at them made me feel as if my heart was being ripped from my chest. Sorrow filled the air as we waved goodbye, hankies tightly gripped in our hands. It felt like torture, sad faces streaked with tears have been forever engraved in my memories. Be that as it may, hope was not lost, contrarily it was present and ready to fill my future. No one knew when we would see each other next but one thing was clear, God's plan for my life was advancing. God's plan always advances, even though sometimes it doesn't appear to or feel like it is. No matter where we are at in our journey, God is in control and His master plan will succeed.

We stepped onto the train carriage, with all our belongings squeezed into five big suitcases. I recall how hectic the atmosphere aboard the crowded train was, people were screaming and pushing to get to their allocated seats. I could hear my dad bellow, 'Watch out boys', as he pushed us forward. The corridor and floor of that train was dirty, and the smell of sweat filled my nostrils. Boarded passengers from all sorts of backgrounds and cultures were trying to reach their cabins. My brother and I laughed as we heard them speak in other languages, this temporary distraction relieved us from the sadness in our hearts. When we finally got to our cabin and sat down, my dad seemed restless as he tackled our luggage into the appropriate baggage space. It was like a game of Tetris, where each object had to fit perfectly within its boundaries. Mum was the opposite; she had a calm assurance about her. As the train set off on its journey and began to gain some speed, I curiously looked out the window. Everything on the outside seemed as if it was chasing after us, moving so fast to the point where I could no longer distinguish the landscape, but instead could only envisage wondrous green, yellow, and brown hues whirling past me.

Momentarily, my sorrow had been forgotten and instead everything struck me as conceivably simple. Although I didn't comprehend the huge sacrifice that we as a family were making, God had already started to teach me one of the most significant lessons you can learn in life – everything has a price, and without sacrifice it cannot be obtained. Sacrifice is a part of our Christian walk. We should not be taken by surprise when God requires it. God the Father has sacrificed his only Son, Jesus, so that we might live. What makes us think that we are not required to sacrifice anything? Sacrifice should happen daily as we live under God's grace and the result of what Jesus has done for us on the cross. Let's never underestimate the concept of sacrifice, as it is so important for believers. Very often, this is the means that God uses to bring us to our destiny. This is the vehicle which carries us towards what God has prepared for us, much like the train that brought my family to Germany. In defiance of the sadness and fear of the unknown, joy would rise in the morning.

Many hours had already passed since we had left the train station at Paola, and now it was lunch time. I can specifically call to mind that lunch as my mother opened the bag containing our sandwiches and drinks. Suddenly, a breathtaking aroma filled our train cabin with the wafting scent of Italian salami that would grip your taste buds. I was so hungry that I devoured the first sandwich like a lion devouring its prey. In an instant, all sadness, and any questions about where we were heading had disappeared. All I wanted was food. I can still hear my mums' gentle words of advice, 'Not so quick Arma, not so quick. Eat slowly otherwise you will feel sick later'. Like a self-fulfilling prophecy, a short time later I did start to feel a bit heavy, so I decided to take a little nap since the journey was long, and we were only at the beginning.

I had no idea how long I had snoozed. As night crept in, I looked around and saw my mom holding my brother in her arms whilst she had her head resting on the neck support of her seat. My dad stood in the corridor smoking, his face showed how tired and worried he was. As an eight-year-old boy, I had no idea what he was thinking. I had never really seen my dad like that. I decided to hop out of my seat and open the cabin door. I threw my arms around his waist and looked up to ask him, 'Are we there yet?' He answered that the journey was going to take a while and that I'd better go and sleep. The corridor window was ajar to let the cigarette smoke escape. I remember a tremendous whistling sound would emerge every time we went through a tunnel, and a gentle breeze of air would tousle my hair as I hugged my dad. I looked up again and asked him to close the window and come with me back into the cabin. He replied, 'You go, I will be there soon'.

It is interesting to note how every significant moment remains engraved in our memory, how we can remember things, smells, and expressions on people's faces so many years later. Going back to my seat, I was wondering why my dad looked preoccupied. Falling asleep that night, I tried to imagine what Germany would be like. I questioned whether I would make new friends and what school would entail. With countless questions and no idea of what to expect or what I was going to encounter, there was no way, shape, or form that I was ready to face all the changes and challenges that I had ahead of me. All I knew was that we were destined to arrive at better place, a bigger and more densely populated city. This was something I had never experienced before as I had grown up in a small village in Italy where I felt invincible and free, and everyone knew each other. There wasn't much traffic, nor many things to think about. I could practically do what I wanted, running through the narrow village thoroughfares, and creating havoc with my friends. Life was comfortable and sweet, but God had a much bigger plan for my family, a plan that would be beneficial not only for me but for the generations to come. There I was, a little boy half asleep in a train cabin, thinking about Germany yet completely clueless of being amidst a life-changing journey.

When morning finally arrived, the first thing I heard as I forced myself to open my eyes were the cries of my little brother. In front of me my mum was stuffing things into our food bag. 'Get ready we are nearly there' my dad directed as he was standing at the cabin door, reaching for our luggage. I noticed how edgy and tired he was, no idea if he had even an ounce of sleep. When I looked outside of the big cabin window, as the train slowed to a stop at our destination, my first observation was that the houses looked different, larger than the houses I was familiar with back in Italy. Meanwhile, there was a lot of noise coming from the corridor as the passengers prepared to disembark from the train. As I stood in the corridor looking at these people, a sense of excitement arose in me. I can still hear my dad saying upon arrival, 'Stay close son, stay close'. 'Grab your mum's hand', he continued while wrestling with the luggage towards the exit.

I looked at her and could see tears flowing down her cheeks. Should I worry? Should I be scared? What was happening? These were the thoughts racing through my mind as fear, anxiety and panic gripped me in the same breath. My mum held my little brother in her arms, with the food bag and her purse in the other, simultaneously dragging me along towards the exit.

The train came to a stop and the passengers started to push each other and fight for a quick exit off the train. The unforgettable smell of old leather and cigarette smoke filled the train walls, and my nostrils as I was carried off the train.

In the distance I saw my fathers red flannelette shirt as he searched for a place to put our luggage down. We made it. We had arrived! I remember hearing through the loudspeakers two out of a multitude of words I did not yet understand; 'Bahnhof' and 'Mannheim'. I had no idea what those words meant. I had an epiphany when I realised that people around me were speaking many different languages. I was so used to only hearing one language at home and in the village, but in Germany everything was strikingly different. Myriads of people ran around the station, holding tightly onto suitcases and all sorts of things. I had never seen so many people in one spot at the same time, nor heard the resounding clatter of so many strange and unknown languages which bounced around in my ears. Even the air smelled different there compared to back home. I surveyed my parents to see why we were at a standstill. All I could see was my dad moving his head from left to right, as if he was waiting to spot someone in the middle of the crowd. Sure enough, a mature couple approached us and initiated a hug from both my parents. I couldn't help but think, who are they? I have never seen them before. Why are they here? As I analysed the situation, the lady knelt to my level and with a broad smile said 'ciao'. The stench of cigarettes was unmanageable, it was so strong that I could hardly breathe. It alluded me to a memory of when my grandfather used to start the fire in our fireplace back home in my village. Regardless of the bad breath, my brain still registered that she had greeted me in a language familiar to me, which filled my heart with joy. Continuing to converse in Italian she said, 'You must be Armando. Your dad has told me a lot about you. Here, have this candy, it's for you'. Without a moment of hesitation, I grabbed it and shoved it in my mouth. Boy was it good. It tasted sweet and sour at the same time, unlike anything I had ever tasted before. As I focused on devouring the delicious candy, my family, along with those strangers moved towards the train station exit. A giant clock directly in front of me caught my attention as I was walking out. The dial was so shiny, and the clock hands were huge. The clock was ticking, although I couldn't hear it. To me it resembled the beginning of a new era.

Even though I had no idea where we were and what life was going to be like for us from then on, God had already prepared everything. As I grew up, God slowly but surely revealed His marvellous plan to me. Little did I know of the difficulties ahead which God would use to shape me in the exact form He wanted me to be, or how much pain this transition was going to cause. One thing I have learned is that it is better not to know what's ahead and learn to simply trust God during the journey, rather than attempting to figure it all out by myself.

> 'Trust in the Lord with all your heart and lean not on your own understanding; in all your ways acknowledge Him, and He shall direct your paths.'
>
> *Proverbs 3:5-6 NKJV*

To 'lean not on your own understanding' is simply another way to express the fact that we need God and faith to live the life He has prepared for us. There are many Biblical examples that illustrate this point.

a) Abraham was 'leaning not on his own understanding' when he was walking with Isaac up the mountain to offer him up a sacrifice to the LORD.

b) Joseph was 'leaning not on his own understanding' when he was thrown in prison for not giving in when his master's wife wanted to sleep with him.

c) Daniel and his friends were 'leaning not on their own understanding' when they were thrown in the fiery furnace for not bowing down to worship other gods.

God created you. He loves you. He knows you better than you will ever know yourself. The fact that He is all-knowing gives Him the ability to see what lies ahead. He knows what is necessary for us to be the person He created us to be. He also knows what needs to take place, and the direction in which we must journey to receive the blessings He wants to give us.

Today as I look back at those times, I thank God for creating the opportunity, and my parents for seizing the opportunity all that time ago to move to Germany. Although I didn't know it then, God was already on the move to prepare a better future for us all. It is imperative to realise that life is never pain free, and that there is always a price to pay for following God's glorious plan for our life.

chapter four
THE CHOICE IS YOURS

Are we, as Christians, willing to pay the price so that the next generation and the generations to come have a real example on how to follow God's plan and purpose? God's desire is for us to flourish and bear much fruit. However, without seeing and accepting God's perfect plan for our lives, it will never happen. Instead of reaping a full reward, we will only receive a half reward.

Behind God's design, there is a mission that needs to be fulfilled. Never view your own life mission as being simple and isolated. God has divinely linked you and your vocation with others, so that when all of us come together and bring to the table what is required, Jesus' bride, the beautiful church will benefit from it.

As expressed earlier, God's plan for our life didn't begin at birth and it won't end at death. God does not organise things at the last minute, He plans way ahead of time. He has a perfect plan for every life, and He calls everyone to that plan. The first difficulty I found when confronted with God's intentions for my life was to accept His plan blindly, with no restrictions.

Around the age of fourteen during a youth camp, God told me that He had set me aside for a great purpose in life. From that moment on, I knew that my destiny would end up differently than how I had planned it. I had discovered that God was calling me to serve Him in a ministry role as mentioned in Ephesians 4:11-13 NIV.

> 'So Christ himself gave the apostles, the prophets, the evangelists, the pastors and teachers, to equip his people for works of service, so that the body of Christ may be built up until we all reach unity in the faith and in the knowledge of the Son of God and become mature, attaining to the whole measure of the fullness of Christ.'

I was happy about the news but on the other hand I knew that meant I could not simply do whatever I wanted anymore. All the dreams I had to become a professional soccer player were suddenly put into question. The battle had begun. I was now confronted with a choice to either accept His plan or not to. In all honesty, I struggled with this choice for several years. My reply was always 'not now God, not now. Let me finish this first and let me also finish this other thing', just like the people mentioned in Luke 9:57-62 NIV.

> 'The Cost of Following Jesus
>
> As they were walking along the road, a man said to him, "I will follow you wherever you go." Jesus replied, "Foxes have dens and birds have nests, but the Son of Man has no place to lay his head." He said to another man, "Follow me." But he replied, "Lord, first let me go and bury my father." Jesus said to him, "Let the dead bury their own dead, but you go and proclaim the kingdom of God." Still another said, "I will follow you, Lord;

> but first let me go back and say goodbye to my family." Jesus replied, "No one who puts a hand to the plow and looks back is fit for service in the kingdom of God."'

As the years passed, that voice inside me remained, persistently asking, 'When will you make your choice?' The voice grew increasingly louder. God is always good. Undeterred by all the things we don't do, He still loves us, and He will not give up on us. I suppressed His voice and delayed making my choice for several years by pursuing my own desires and ideas. Deep down I knew very well that eventually I would be forced to make this decision. Some people have received God's plan for their lives while others have gone their own way and done whatever they pleased. They don't want the will of God, and they don't seek for it. As for me, the question lingered. At the age of eighteen, I was at a crossroad, having to decide between my forever dream to become a professional soccer player, or trust God to transform me to become all He wanted me to be. I'm glad I made the superior choice to follow God's plan.

Following God's purpose for your life is always the best thing to do.

One Bible verse that has helped me every time when I've had to make a choice is found in Proverbs 19:21 NIV, and it reads, 'Many are the plans in a person's heart, but it is the LORD's purpose that prevails'. God's plan for our life is impeccable, suiting us perfectly. It matures us to become all that God had intended us to be. That doesn't mean He expects us to be perfect, He knows we won't be. He does expect that while we're here on earth, we strive to the best of our abilities to be more like Him, growing in wisdom and learning from our mistakes. One thing I have learned is that the true test of a person's spiritual life and character is not what he does in the amazing moments of life, but what he does during the ordinary times, when there is nothing exciting happening. God's plans not only unfold during the exciting moments in life, but also during the hard and seemingly unimportant times. God's plan constantly develops throughout our entire life. We advance from stage to stage, milestone to milestone. In other words, God's plan does not unfold in a one-time action but in stages over the course of our life.

Therefore, it is vital to our progress to kill the second man constantly, every single day. We must not forget that the second man is dangerous; he is the one who can end God's plan if we allow him to, he is the one who causes us the most struggles in life. Hence why the Bible speaks so openly about him, instructing us on how to handle him.

Everything we do in life is dependent on the choices we make. A choice has the power to make us or break us. Our existence comprises of choices that we make. Whether we feel it immediately or not, our life is being shaped by the choices we are making in the present. Choices establish a pattern and a foundation for our life. In view of the significant impact that every choice has on our lives in the present and the future, we cannot allow the second man to have the upper hand on this matter. We must fight him because if we let the second man take control of our life, he will lead us astray and will negatively influence our choices. Step by step he aims to make us drift from what God has in store for us, that's his nature.

I had to fight against the second man bigtime. I was struggling with deciding whether to accept God's plan for my life or my own. I asked myself the same question over and over, 'If I accept the plan of God, what are the consequences? What would I need to give up?' The first time I had accepted Jesus in my heart was around the age of nine during a Sunday School service. I did not fully understand what it all meant at such a young age, however, several years later at the age of thirteen I renewed that decision. This time I was committed to understanding this momentous decision in more detail. I recall my old pastor preaching about putting off the second man and putting on the new nature, and something in me was hungry to know more about that subject. Even at this age I wanted to grasp this divine concept, without knowing of its paramount importance in leading a Christian life. I started to enquire what it entailed to put off the second man and put on the new nature in Christ.

Years passed and I began to comprehend that there are several major points on this matter that require our attention. To begin with, everyone that goes on this journey will need to make the conscious and continual choice of refusing to let the second man lead his life. After this initial decision, it is vital to be aware that the second man will not give up his leading position readily. He will stand his ground and fight till the bitter end. This fight is not an easy one but it's necessary to progress in our Christian walk, so it is important that we understand how to approach it. Before we go there, it is critical to go one step back and reflect on how we are made and how we function as a human being.

I took a lot of joy in and practiced several fighting sports in my youth: kick boxing, Thai boxing, and freestyle (what we call MMA today). One lesson they all had in common was that before you can engage in a fight, you better know who you are and what your limits are. Even though this lesson might seem of less importance, let me tell you friends that this fight is the one that determines whether you win or lose. You might have heard the expression 'as in the natural, so in the spiritual'. Well, that is accurate. In a fight, knowing who you are and what you can do is indispensable. Without this understanding we have lost before we have even started. This leaves us asking the pressing question 'who am I?' We can discover the answer for ourselves in the Word of God.

> 'So God created human beings in his own image. In the image of God, he created them; male and female he created them'.

Genesis 1:27 NIV

What does this piece of Scripture mean? The Bible teaches us that we are a three-dimensional being, having been made with a body, spirit, and soul. This already gives us an indication that we will be fighting on these three fronts. I'll explain this topic in more detail later in the book.

chapter five
THE FIGHT

When does the fight begin? This is the primary question at the forefront of our mind. The fight will start immediately at our conversion, the moment we decide to follow Jesus and go against our second man – our sinful nature.

Paul articulated in his letter to Galatians, verse 2:20 NLT that [his] 'old self has been crucified with Christ. It is no longer I who live, but Christ lives in me. So, I live in this earthly body by trusting in the Son of God, who loved me and gave himself for me'.

Understanding what happens at our conversion is important so we'll be able to determine the next move in our fight. At our conversion, we acknowledge four important truths.

1. Believe in the sacrifice of Jesus accomplished on the Cross.

2. We repent from our old ways and ask forgiveness for our sins.
3. We accept and confess Jesus as our Saviour and King.
4. Jesus comes into our life, forgives us from our sins, and we are born again.
   We become a new creation.

It is through Christ that we are born again. Since we are born of Adam, we inherit his sinful nature; but since we are now born again in Christ, we inherit a new nature. To mention 2 Corinthians 5:17 again, 'Therefore, if anyone is in Christ, he is a new creation'. We don't lose our sinful nature once we receive Christ. The Bible says that the sinful nature remains in us until the end of our days here on earth. This is why the fight between the old and the new nature is relentless throughout our entire life. We will struggle and we will fail, but we will often win. We will win because of He who is in us, strengthening us every day, if we let Him. At conversion, the Spirit of God takes up residence in each believer and supplies the power we need to overcome the pull of the sinful nature within us. Now that the second man must reside with the new man, the fight is now on!

> 'For the desires of the flesh are against the Spirit, and the desires of the Spirit are against the flesh, for these are opposed to each other, to keep you from doing the things you want to do.'
>
> *Galatians 5:17 ESV*

As we learned earlier, we don't lose our sinful nature once we receive Christ. Both the old and the new natures must now live together in the same body. In fact, the old natural man doesn't like the new man, since both have complete opposite natures, desires, and agendas.

We need to understand that before we became a follower of Jesus, the natural man ruled our thoughts, desires, and our actions. In other terms he was the boss, and he doesn't want to surrender his power to submit to the new master. Our goal is to overcome and kill the second man, and let the spiritual man take control. John the Baptist proclaimed that '[Jesus] must become greater and greater in us, and I must become less and less' (John 3:30 NLT).

Now that we know when the fight starts, it is of utmost importance to understand why we must fight. The bottom line is that if we don't fight, there will be no change in our life. We will not grow spiritually, nor be able to do the things of the spirit, two fundamental things that Jesus has commanded us to do.

Why do we have to fight?

The Bible explains that the reason for fighting is due to our sinful nature. The Bible speaks of sinful flesh. In fact, Romans 6:6-7 NIV speaks of 'the body ruled by sin'. The sinful nature in all of humanity is universal. Everyone has a sinful nature which affects every part of us.

Where did the sin nature come from?

The Bible says that God created humans good and without a sinful nature.

> 'God created man in His own image, in the image of God he created him; male and female he created them.'
>
> *Genesis 1:27 ESV*

> 'God saw all that he had made, and it was very good.'
>
> *Genesis 1:31*

However, Genesis 3 records the disobedience of Adam and Eve. With one wrong action, sin entered their nature. Genesis 3:8-10 describes that they were immediately troubled with a sense of shame, and so they hid from God's presence. Genesis 5:3 mentions that when they had children, Adam's image and likeness was passed along to his offspring.

> 'Therefore, just as sin entered the world through one man, and death through sin, and in this way death came to all people, because all sinned—'
>
> *Romans 5:12 NIV*

The result is separation between man and God the Creator. There is only one Person in the history of the world who did not have a sinful nature: Jesus Christ. Jesus lived a completely sinless life. He was 'the Holy and Righteous One' described in Acts 3:14, and the one who 'had no sin' as mentioned in 2 Corinthians 5:21. This allowed Jesus to be sacrificed on the cross as our perfect substitute, 'a lamb without blemish or defect' (read 1 Peter 1:18-19 NIV). This was the ultimate price to pay, so that mankind can return to God through repentance and experience a conversion, a rebirth, with a new purpose and everlasting life. Once we have discovered when and why the fights starts, we need to focus on the question, 'How am I supposed to fight?'

Alone we're not able to automatically allow our new nature to take over, it is a step-by-step procedure. The key is to let God constantly grow in us so that the new man gets stronger, to overcome the fight against the second man. We cannot allow for the second man to lead our lives anymore. It's Jesus who should be in control and steer our new man.

Working in collaboration with Jesus is integral so that our new nature will always prevail. The great Apostle Paul informs us to, 'Put on your new nature, created to be like God — truly righteous and holy' (read Ephesians 4:22-24). Colossians 3:10 NLT instructs us to, 'Put on your new nature, and be renewed as you learn to know your Creator and become like him.'

If we follow Jesus and put these verses into practice, we will be able to feed our new nature, become strong, and live as overcomers. If we are unwilling to put in the work, the second man will gain strength and endeavour to prevail over our new nature. You can feed your spirit man, or you can feed your flesh. Just remember that whichever one you feed more will win. If you want something to grow, feed it. If you want something to die off, then starve it. You get good at walking in the Spirit the same way you get good at walking in the flesh… with practice.

I became proficient at playing soccer because I trained every day. It was not an accident. Let me tell you, it was not always fun to practice. I threatened to quit more than once, but my desire to become a professional player was greater than the temporary suffering.

Furthermore, you'll need to have a goal and persist at it until you have reached that goal. What should that goal be? To be more and more like Jesus. Walking in the Spirit is the same, the more you practice, the better you get at it. I made many wrong turns before

I managed to stay on the right track. You might take some wrong turns yourself, but the only way to get back on track is with pure diligence and determination.

The more you pray, the easier it gets. The more you read the Word, the easier it gets to read the Word without being distracted by your endless task list. Walking in the flesh is similar, if you keep at it, you can get very good. It can become second nature so that walking in the Spirit seems abnormal and sinning seems normal.

People who want to change their bodies often change their diet to get the desired results. Sometimes when we look at ourselves and don't like where we are at, we may consider a change in our spiritual diet. Romans 8:14 ESV explains that '…all who are led by the Spirit of God are sons of God'. We need to be led by the Spirit of God whilst we are training and growing our Spiritual man. In our Christian walk, we will have to conquer many things which will only happen through combat. The Good news is that Jesus has not left us alone fighting our battles. He is always with us. As we put His teaching into practice in our personal life, our spiritual man will get stronger and defeat the natural man.

> **Whichever one you feed more will win.**

The Bible says that 'in all these things we are more than conquerors through him who loved us' (Romans 8:37 ESV), and that we 'can do all things through Christ, who strengthens me'. (Philippians 4:13 NKJV). Killing the second man is not an easy task, but more than that, God has given us all the tools necessary to accomplish the task at hand. There is no excuse for us to not prevail and overcome. The emphasis in the next chapter will focus on how we can upgrade our fighting skills and abilities and learn what tools we have at hand. Additionally, you will gain an understanding of how the enemy works, recognising his schemes and tactics, in preparation for a counterattack.

chapter six
UNDERSTANDING THE BATTLEFIELD

The Battlefield is where everything happens. It's the place where we decide whether we choose to live a life that is half spiritual and half fleshly, or one or the other fully. This is simply because it is in this place, where our actions are determined and put into practice.

In the moment of our conversion, we received Christ and are assured of our salvation. We must ensure that our hearts remain in right standing with God and diligently continue in our commitment to follow Him. It is precisely for this reason that it is vital to understand the battlefield ahead of time to grasp how to move in it. Subsequently, navigation through the battlefield will be easier whilst in battle as we commit to following Him. The battlefield is the scene where our spiritual warfare transpires, the place where the second man wrestles the new man. It's also where the enemy comes to attack us. Some say that it's in our mind, some say it's deep within our soul. Either way it is crucial to recognise and know your battlefield.

Our battlefield embraces our thoughts, imagination, reasoning, and intellect, as well as our emotions and will. In all these aspects lie the very heart of an individual. By our thoughts and feelings, we determine our will and purpose for our lives. As Christians, we seek to live by the truth and power of God because they are our assurance of God's promised victory in every single situation in life. We are not ignorant of the reality of evil and the destruction that surrounds our world daily. It is in this process that we will encounter a very real spiritual struggle in our thoughts, emotions and will. The adversary knows that these areas are directly related to the power of our faith and the means to receiving the promises of God. The adversary's goal is to weaken the faith of every Christian by meeting him at the usual place – the battlefield.

Man is a very complex creation. In late 2016, I learned one of the most valuable lessons of my Christian life.

I was carrying out a forty-day full fast. It was something that I had dreamed of doing since I was thirteen years old, a life desire that God had put into my heart since that young age. The fulfillment of this desire occurred many years later when I had just turned forty.

What did I learn during this fast? I learned how God created us physically, emotionally, and spiritually. I discovered a great complexity in understanding how God has created us; the reasons why we were made exactly this way are multifaceted. To discover and fathom these things will only work to our advantage and benefit. When you have a deep understanding of who you are, how you function and what makes you tick, you then discover your real strengths and weaknesses. Consequently, your whole life changes accordingly.

You may inquire why this is important to know, and what this has this to do with being acquainted with the battlefield. Let me explain my findings and conclusions. If you only know the battlefield and not yourself, you'll have difficulties moving through the battleground. You'll be slower, more vulnerable and have a disposition of failure. This reaffirms the necessity of knowing yourself and knowing the battleground in preparation for your fashioning into a fearless warrior. In a fight, it is invaluable and a great advantage to understand who you are and what you're capable of. Without this understanding, we have potentially lost before we have even started.

Presently, we will explore more information I have learned during my fast, and obviously looking at what the Bible says on these topics.

> 'So God created human beings in his own image. In the image of God, he created them; male and female he created them.'
>
> *Genesis 1:27 NLT*

What does this mean? We are a Three-dimensional being consisting of Body, Spirit, and Soul.

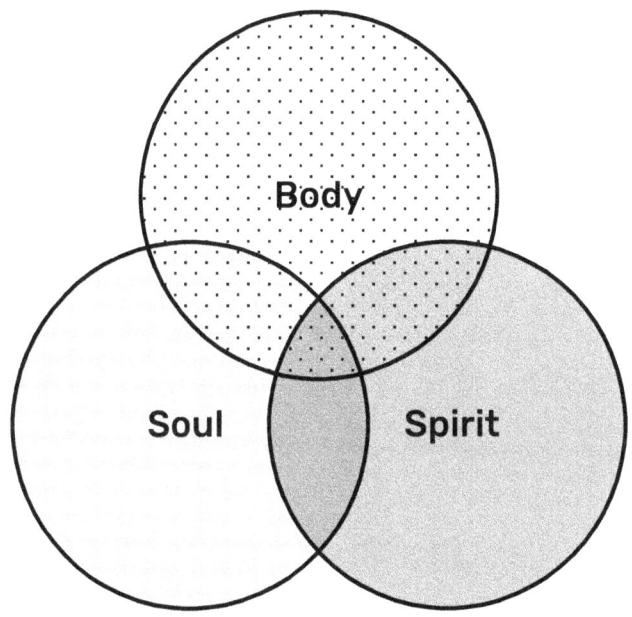

<u>Our Body</u>

It is our body that communicates with the external world. In other words, it is through your body that people recognise you, but this is also the place where we may need to fight some of our battles. At times it will be the enemy attacking us here, other times it may be different factors. There is no doubt whatsoever in my mind about the devil using this battleground to destroy society by setting up all sorts of false standards and pretexts for people to follow. In current times, there are so many controversial and false informational sources telling us how we should look, dress, act etc., which is beyond ridiculous. The media is full nonsense, persuading people with what they believe is right or wrong for us. Low self-esteem issues in many people derive from society's distorted view of acceptable body image. It is God's point of view that we must value and follow. Observe and meditate on these two very powerful statements.

1. Our Body is Perfect

> 'You made all the delicate, inner parts of my body and knit me together in my mother's womb. Thank you for making me so wonderfully complex! Your workmanship is marvellous —how well I know it.'
>
> *Psalm 139:13-14 NLT*

2. We're the Temple of the Holy Spirit

> 'Don't you realize that your body is the temple of the Holy Spirit, who lives in you and was given to you by God? You do not belong to yourself, for God bought you with a high price. So you must honour God with your body.'
>
> *1 Corinthians 6:19-20 NLT*

We live by the book, the Bible. From there we extract our guidelines, wisdom and clarity of what God thinks and says about us. God loves us, and desires for us to always be well. Therefore, let's always listen to what He has to say and take good care of the body He has given us.

> 'How precious also are Your thoughts to me, O God! How great is the sum of them!'
>
> *Psalm 139:17 NKJV*

Our Spirit

> 'Then the LORD God formed the man from the dust of the ground. He breathed the breath of life into the man's nostrils, and the man became a living person.'
>
> *Genesis 2:7 NLT*

Man is more than dust or physical substance. God is the Source of life, and He directly placed life within man. We can picture it this way — Adam's body had just been formed by God from the dust of the earth, a lifeless human body lying on the ground. Then God leaned over and 'breathed' His own 'breath of life' into the man's nostrils. Two things occurred here, one being that God gave man a spirit. Secondly, God gave man a soul. Mankind received a double portion of God and became a living soul. Why do you think mankind needed both a spirit and a soul?

Our spirit is the life and power of God, given to man to animate him. The Hebrew word for spirit is *ruach* which means wind, breath, air, spirit.

The spirit is part of the very essence of God and is designed to return to Him once mankind dies.

Another reason we require a spirit is so that God can communicate with us. The apostle Paul confirms this in Romans 8:16 NIV, 'The Spirit himself testifies with our spirit that we are God's children'. Our spirit plays a considerable role in our life and everything we do is dependent on it. I will explain this later in more detail.

> 'Yes, remember your Creator now while you are young, before the silver cord of life snaps and the golden bowl is broken. Don't wait until the water jar is smashed at the spring and the pulley is broken at the well. For then the dust will return to the earth, and the spirit will return to God who gave it.'

Ecclesiastes 12:6-7 NLT

Our Soul

The soul is who we are. It is the invisible part of us that identifies us as a person. God has given every person a unique soul/identity. This is the centre of our being – the part that lives forever – that either goes to heaven or hell after we die.

The word soul in Hebrew is *nephesh*: an animated, breathing, conscious, and living being. Man did not become a living soul until God breathed life into him.

> 'Jesus replied: "Love the Lord your God with all your heart and with all your soul and with all your mind"'
>
> *Matthew 22:37 NIV*

As a physical, animate, rational, and spiritual being, man is unique among all living things upon the earth. The Bible says that the devil comes '…only to steal and kill and destroy; I [Jesus] have come that they may have life and have it to the full' (John 10:10 NIV). Where do you think the enemy will go to attack you? On the battlefield of course. Which areas do you think he will attack? Your whole being. Sometimes it will be your body, your soul or your spirit, and other times it may be a combination of two or all three areas.

When we look at the story of Job in the Old Testament, we learn that God allowed the devil to attack Job on all three levels: body, soul, and spirit. The first strike was at Jobs' possessions, then he killed his sons and daughters, to then attack Jobs' health directly. Ultimately, the devil's goal was to destroy Job's faith, but he was unsuccessful. Job was able to stand in battle because he knew his battlefield, and he knew himself, but above anything else, he knew his God. He knew that his God would not abandon him. This made Job a champion on the battlefield. Please keep in mind that the victory did not come without paying the price. He felt pain, sorrow, and oppression on the battlefield. There were moments where he struggled and felt like giving up. Yet he chose to stand firm and trust in God.

Another similar example when the enemy employed the same offense strategy was with Jesus, when he tempted Him in the desert.

> 'And when He [Jesus] had fasted forty days and forty nights, afterward He was hungry. Now when the tempter came to Him, he said, "If You are the Son of God, command that these stones become bread."'
>
> Matthew 4:1-3 NKJV

This was an attack on the body via physical hunger. In verse 4, we read about Jesus' counterattack by reciting Deuteronomy 8:3.

> 'But He answered and said, "It is written, 'Man shall not live by bread alone, but by every word that proceeds from the mouth of God.'"'

The devil didn't stop there? No, of course not. Verses 5 and 6 read:

> 'Then the devil took him to the holy city, Jerusalem, to the highest point of the Temple, and said, "If you are the Son of God, jump off! For the Scriptures say,

> 'He will order his angels to protect you.
> And they will hold you up with their hands, so you won't even hurt your foot on a stone.'" (NLT)

What was the devil trying to do here? Trying to crush Jesus's spirit. Of course Jesus knew that what the devil was proposing could have been done, but Jesus knowing the Scriptures in his spirit responded, "'The Scriptures also say, 'You must not test the Lord your God'"' (v.7 NLT). Did the temptations end there? No, as we read on, we can see how the enemy proceeded to attack the soul.

> 'Next the devil took him to the peak of a very high mountain and showed him all the kingdoms of the world and their glory. "I will give it all to you," he said, "if you will kneel down and worship me"' (v. 8-9 NLT).

The notion of possessing everything and being fulfilled by material things is like a sugar shot for the soul. Jesus did not fall into the trap because we read his powerful response in verses 10 through 11.

> '"Get out of here, Satan," Jesus told him "For the Scriptures say, 'You must worship the Lord your God and serve only him.'" Then the devil went away, and angels came and took care of Jesus.'

We must stand our ground first, by knowing ourselves, the battleground, and our God. By doing so, we will be more than overcomers.

> '...everyone born of God overcomes the world. This is the victory that has overcome the world, even our faith. Who is it that overcomes the world? Only the one who believes that Jesus is the Son of God.'
>
> *1 John 5:4-5 NIV*

> '...in all these things we are more than conquerors through him who loved us.'
>
> *Romans 8:37 NIV*

Having this awareness and a progressive knowledge of who we are, we will be able to move and fight victoriously on the battlefield. It will be much more difficult for the devil to attempt to take us down. There is another equally important lesson to learn which is on how to strengthen the new man, your spirit, on the battlefield so that he does not become weak, weary, and risk losing the fight to the second man. To clarify, the battle will always be on the battleground. The difference is that sometimes we will fight the devil and other times we will fight our own second man. To be a winner in both circumstances, we must constantly be working on strengthening our new spiritual man.

During my fast I was weak physically, mentally, and emotionally, although I have never felt better in my entire life as I felt then. You're probably thinking of how that's possible as I didn't eat for forty days straight. Truthfully, my mind was sharper than ever, and my body felt great. I could understand God's Word like never before. All the biblical teachings were now so clear to me, and I was able to hear and distinguish God's voice like never before. It was simply incredible. The question remains, how was this possible? During the whole fast I learned that if we strengthen the spiritual man with prayer, reading and listening to God's voice to our maximum ability, he grows exponentially big in us. This allows Him to steer and lead us to be in alignment with His ways, and to walk in His righteousness. This means that God gains control of our whole entity, guided and safe under God's supervision. This of course does not mean that we suddenly become perfect but simply that God becomes bigger in us, giving us the ability to authoritatively kill the second man. This gives us the possibility and freedom to walk in the light of God in a much more powerful and fruitful way, able to do the things He asks of us with ease. Believe me when I say that when the spiritual man leads our life, it's a completely different spiritual life experience. Our body and soul bow to him and follow in obedience. They feel refreshed and full. Your whole being goes to another dimension. I had never experienced such a thing before the fast, and I have not experienced anything like that since. That's alright though because I know that was a special dispensational time for me in which God had to do several things and reveal to me some other things, and so He created this special, personalised opportunity.

I believe that in some way, God made me experience what Adam and Eve must have felt like in the garden of Eden. It was an exhilarating atmosphere of being one with God, walking and being fully integrated before the presence of God himself. That wonderful experience changed my life on many levels that I would have never dreamed of before starting the fast. This encounter gave me the possibility to learn some core Christian principles that I may have never learned otherwise.

Always remember who God is. Above all, He is our source of life, strength, and power. Yes, it's important to know the battlefield and to understand ourselves, as well as the schemes, tactics and lies of the enemy so that we are well-equipped for battle. More than that, we must never underestimate and fail to remember that without God, we can do nothing.

> 'I can do all things, through Christ that strengthens me….'
>
> Philippians 4:13 NKJV

The Apostle Paul is with no doubt the master apostle when it comes to the subject of killing the second man. As Christians we have a good fight to fight, and through Paul's writings we can discover all the things that God wants to teach us.

> 'Fight the good fight of the faith. Take hold of the eternal life to which you were called when you made your good confession in the presence of many witnesses.'
>
> *1 Timothy 6:12 NIV*

chapter seven
ENTERING THE NEW EL DORADO

I am always amazed and fascinated by how our brain can store all types of our lived emotions and experiences, no matter whether they are good or bad. When I close my eyes and think back, I'm immediately catapulted back to the train station parking lot in Mannheim Germany in 1983. It's as if it is branded in my front lobe. I firmly believe that this event which I call Entering the New Eldorado, has been in the spiritual, a very important milestone in God's divine plan that He set in my life to reach. The best thing about it is the fact that God creates the milestone and then he helps us reach it. This often happens without us knowing it.

Decades later, I have come to realise how God led my entire family through an intricate obstacle course to reach our destiny. Like a road map, I am able to trace every milestone we reached, and I see how everything was interlinked and connected. What once seemed to be an insignificant event in life, is much more than that when viewing it in the spiritual. In hindsight it's easier to figure out why God has allowed you to go through certain things, both pleasurable and unpleasurable, and why some things had to happen first and others later. When we look through God's lens, we can suddenly visualise how God is working in our life, even when we thought nothing was happening. Every detail of our life is in God's hands and is profoundly well planned by Him.

> 'The steps of a man are established by the LORD, when he delights in his way; though he falls, he shall not be cast headlong, for the LORD upholds his hand.'
>
> *Psalm 37:23-24 ESV*

God has always had a unique plan for every one of us, and He will never let that plan fail so long as we collaborate with Him to fulfill it.

> '"For I know the plans I have for you," declares the Lord, "plans to prosper you and not to harm you, plans to give you hope and a future.'
>
> *Jeremiah 29:11 NIV*

I know this is a verse that we quote so often in Christian circles, but do we really understand it? Do we really understand the depths of this snippet of Scripture? I have learned that the only way to collaborate with Him is by living the experience of being led by God through His plan. This will cost us tears, sweat, pain, joy, and so much more. I can also tell you that although it comes at a price, it's worth going through it with God and letting Him completely transform us in the process.

Back to my arrival story in Germany. We were trying to fit all our suitcases into our family friends' car, which took my dad and his friend quite a while until they got everything to fit everything in the boot. It was kind of funny. While this was happening, I waited next to my mum unsure of what to do so I simply observed. I remember thinking about where we were going next. I knew that Dad had managed to obtain a flat for us to live in, but I had no idea where or what it looked like. As I looked around, still fascinated by the big clock at the station tower, I watched every minute pass. Even though the clock arms would move, it seemed that time was standing still.

Finally, we were seated in the car, destination set for our new home. All the sorrow of leaving my little village temporarily vanished due to excitement. It was only later when that sadness and sorrow returned — it would not leave me so easily for a while to come. Driving through the seemingly vast roads was thrilling. Everything appeared so unreal and yet tangible. All I could see were buildings, cars, and many people. Nothing was like what I had always known, and unconsciously, a strange fear started to make itself known.

Dad exclaimed, 'We are here guys, this is it!' All I could see was an old grey building with many windows towering over us; the surrounding area wasn't visually pleasing. One detail I recall vividly is a big, blue sign on the building wall right next to the entrance door displaying the alphanumeric characters B6,1A.

When dad noticed me looking at it, he knelt and said, 'Armando this is our new address, remember these numbers and letters because they are very important'. Dad and his friend started to unload our suitcases from the car as my mum, little brother and I were trying to figure out what to do. Observing the street from every angle I could, I was once again reminded that nothing was ever going to be like it once was. This was a new country, so everything was unfamiliar and strange to me compared to what I was used to. From the streets and the amount of people around, to the smell of the air, everything was different. This was certainly a new chapter.

Standing in front of the enormous, brown wooden entrance door, I was full of excitement and joy. I noted that Dad was relieved but Mum not so much. For some reason she looked worried. With everyone's hands full of luggage, Dad led the way through a huge concrete corridor that eventually led to an inside courtyard. I could see kids' bikes and a few toys in the courtyard, which was already a good sign for me. Suddenly he exclaimed, 'This is ours!' as he pointed with his finger towards a painted white façade, with one window at the front and a small open porch. The main entrance to the flat was a green metal door on the inside of the porch. As Dad opened the door, I was inundated with a multitude of emotions. I didn't know what to think or do so I let out a liberatory cry. My mum ran to me quickly and hugged me whilst ensuring me that everything was going to be alright. After crying for a while, I felt lighter. However, once the tears had passed, I was finally able to enjoy the move into our long-awaited new home.

Everyone was busy moving stuff around, and other friends had also joined in the effort to help us get settled in. Some of them also brought food and gifts for us. For a moment it felt like a joyous Christmas atmosphere. My little brother and I ran around and exploring each room. I can still recall the layout of the house. Upon entering through the main door, you were greeted into an open-concept kitchen and living. Behind were two bedrooms, one for my parents and the other for us boys. Our beds were already in position. In the corridor between the two rooms was a bathroom, and to my surprise there was only a tiny sink and bathtub, no toilet. My brother and I kept exploring the flat, but the location of the toilet was a mystery which kept us busy for a short time, but we eventually discovered that it was inside the porch area. Whilst we were scrutinising every detail of our new place, the adults were having fun, laughing, and conversing with one another. As evening approached, everyone returned to their own homes, as Mum got us ready for bed. What a day it was, a full assortment of emotions and feelings. It was surreal and strange. The thought settled in that this new chapter in our lives began right here.

During the first week, my parents were constantly busy sorting the house, and running back and forth into town to sort out our paperwork. I went to explore the courtyard further and was able to meet some of the other kids who lived there. To my surprise a few of them spoke Italian as well, so communicating was easy for us. Other kids spoke foreign languages to me, but this did not stop us from playing together. One evening, my mum asked me as she was putting my brother and I to bed, 'Do you want to go to school as you used back home?' 'Yes!' I answered without any hesitation. 'That's great, you will go in just two sleeps', my mum replied. My 'yes' was linked to positive memories, ones of familiarity and joy. Little did I know that I would have to learn to adjust and fit into this new environment, and it wasn't going to be as easy as I had innocently thought.

You see, sometimes we do the exact same thing in our Christian walk. God is trying to teach us new things and learn to walk in His ways, but instead of being fully led by Him into transforming into this new man, we pull the breaks. We compare this new information we're receiving to what we already know and are familiar with. We try in our own might to fit God's plans and purposes for our lives through our lens, not His. Doing things in our own strength is to our own detriment because it means that God has more work to do in us to help with unlearning certain things, for the purpose of teaching us new, true, and righteous things. Let me encourage you friends to follow God with no hesitation. Yes, use what you know, and what you have learned in the past, just be sure to always be willing to learn and explore new things in God.

My first day at school was a very dramatic experience. Together with Mum and my little brother Stefano, we arrived very early in front of this humongous, light brown building. It had a massive courtyard surrounded by plenty of trees I could climb on. Without any warning, an incredibly loud bell sounded. It was so loud that I couldn't hear a single word that Mum was saying to me, I simply followed her lead as she pulled on my arm. As we entered school, a lady was waiting for us with a big smile. She shook our hands and indicated for us to follow her. She was going to be my elementary teacher for the next five years. Her name? Frau Busse. Initially I disliked her, but with time I became aware of how understanding, inclusive and capable she was. I still thank God for her today; she was instrumentally used by Him during my whole troubled time at elementary school, and I don't know where I would be today if she hadn't been there for me then.

I found myself standing in front of a classroom full of other kids that looked nothing like me. They all spoke a language, German, that I didn't understand yet. My mum had now gone home, and I went into full panic mode and started to cry, calling out for my mum. With the classroom door closed I felt trapped, I had nowhere to go. All my classmates were looking at me, and I felt so embarrassed and awkward. Frau Busse simply looked at me and smiled. Strangely enough, looking into her light brown eyes would calm me down. After a while, she took me by the hand and led me to my seat next to another boy. Frau Busse kept saying things to me with a smile, but I couldn't understand a word she was saying. This would really frustrate the life out of me, and a lot of anger built up inside of me, without my knowing it. I could only guess by her gestures what she was saying. She kept pointing to the boy sitting next to me and repeating his name, Domenico. To my surprise Domenico began to talk to me in Italian. What a relief it was to know that I could finally converse with someone in my own language. From that day, we became best friends in elementary school. He spoke both German and Italian well, so he gave me a tour around the whole school and introduced me to other kids. I spent my school hours staring at the walls and daydreaming. I couldn't focus because I did not understand a word the teachers or pupils said to me, yet Frau Busse was always there, patient and smiling. Weeks and months passed, and the situation was always the same. I came home from school crying and frustrated to the max. I shouted out in frustration to my mum, 'Why did you bring me here? Why can't we go back home? I hate it here'. She was lost for words, her eyes full of tears. I had no idea what battles she was simultaneously facing. In the end, we were all in the same boat trying to make it work. Obviously being so young, I could not see far beyond what was happening in my own world.

This is comparable to what sometimes happens in our Christian walk. We can be so focused on our own little world that we don't see what God is doing within the bigger picture. We tend to blame God when we find ourselves in certain situations, not seeing that it is all ultimately part of God's divine plan.

Initially, this abrupt change of environment did not really scare me, as I was born with an adventurous spirit. Adjusting to a new life is not easy, in my case it was moving to a different country with a different language, people, customs, food, and many other things. You don't realise in your youth all the changes that will inevitably come your way. It can be challenging when you find yourself in a situation facing major changes to your usual way of life. In defiance of pain and tears, by grasping that fact God has everything under control and that He can use these situations for good, we will then be able to comprehend the main principle for Christian growth.

> '...we know that God causes everything to work together for the good of those who love God and are called according to his purpose for them.'
>
> *Romans 8:28 NLT*

For us to grow and for God to enlarge our capacity, He must stretch us every now and then. It's not an easy process, it hurts but it's all part of spiritual maturation and a deeper understanding and relationship with God. It is through this exact process that God strengthens our spiritual man to be able to fight and kill the second man.

One full year had now passed since we had migrated from our tiny village in Italy to Mannheim in Germany. Everything had now been grounded in a sense of familiarity, and a routine had installed itself. Everything seemed fine on the surface; I made many friends, became proficient in German, therefore communicating was no longer a problem. In fact, I had become rather cocky in my communication style.

Like a rock, Frau Busse was always there and always willing to help. She stayed back after school with me countless times re-teaching everything that was taught in class earlier that day. She really tried everything she could to help me. She even assured my parents time and again that I would eventually come to a positive turning point soon.

One day as I arrived home from school, something unexpected happened. I found some strange people sitting and talking to my mum, with books stacked on the table. Everyone was friendly and they spoke Italian fluently. I observed a charismatic quality about them, but I was unable to explain it. They would speak about God and Jesus and sing together with Mum. These gatherings continued for weeks where they would come and evangelise to her. They were born again Italian Christians in Germany. God's ways sometimes make me laugh. Mum seemed different, much happier. She sang joyfully, and I wouldn't see her cry as often. I wondered what had transpired in these past few weeks that led to this sudden change.

One evening at the dinner table, a huge argument broke out between my parents. Dad was disgruntled, voicing that he was fed up with religion, Jesus, and with these people always showing up at our house. Meanwhile, Mum was trying to explain that it wasn't a religion but rather a personal relationship with God. The atmosphere was electric, the room filled with clamour and tears shed by everyone. I couldn't figure out why Dad was so against Mum on this topic. For several weeks to follow, the Italian Christians did not show up at our house. Regardless of that, my mum persisted praying on her knees every single day as well as actively reading the Bible. It evidently did her a world of good. As she persisted in prayer and supplication before God, she received her victory; a few months later Dad unexpectedly changed his mind and gave her the ok to go to church and follow her God. He would exclaim every Sunday that, 'If you go to church, you will take the kids with you'.

As Mum devoted herself to go to church with us consistently every Sunday, she began to live out her Christian faith to the full. I was secretly captivated by the music and the singers and enjoyed seeing the large smiles on people's faces. I would attend Sunday School — a place of fun, laughter, and biblical teaching. Along with the other children we played games, spoke about God and the Bible, and enjoyed our time together. The teachers were always nice, I remember them organising competitions with a winner's gift. I loved competitions, and I always wanted to win. Little did I know that through these small, cherished moments of our lives, God's plan for my family and I was advancing. God was leading us towards the desired milestone. Even though I continued going to church every Sunday, my experience with God always remained neutral, maybe even superficial. Yes, I enjoyed going, but I also loved doing my own things.

Several years passed as we simply cruised along as a family unit. Living in Germany had become the new norm and we were well integrated. My parents would work at their respective jobs, and my younger brother and I would go to school. The only thing lacking was that dad still refused to come to church with us. My mum reaffirmed, 'Don't worry, one day God will touch him, you'll see'. That's exactly what happened. One Sunday, Dad miraculously decided to join us at church, and God moved in a way that only He can. I had never seen my dad like this. He changed radically for Christ in a way that no one could have ever imagined. He lost friends because of Christ and suffered injustices because of the gospel. This didn't dissuade him in his faith. His experience with God had been so strong that nothing shook him. At last, he had become a follower of Christ, radically saved, and transformed. Be mindful of the fact that it's not because your parents become followers of Jesus that the children will automatically follow in sequence. We must all make a momentous decision at one point in our lives regarding our salvation. The choice of salvation is purely personal and cannot depend on anyone else. The responsibility of our salvation is entirely ours.

Skipping ahead to the age of thirteen, I liked my life. I was bold, adventurous, and felt like the king of the world. My peers were amicable and enjoyed being around me. A few people around me at this time acknowledged leadership on my life and others would oppose, suggesting that I will never amount to much. I was very boisterous at school — that anger that we spoke earlier had not left me, contrarily it had been amplified — my answer to everything was violence. It made me feel strong and safe, it was an erroneous frame of mind. I would rarely pay attention in class, let alone study, yet I always managed to pass my exams. My parents were called into the principal's office weekly to hear and discuss all my wrongdoings. The anger that began to brew in me many years ago now felt a part of me. To this day, I believe that our move from Italy to Germany contributed to the development of this anger, even though I know wholeheartedly that it was God's will for me personally, and for my entire family.

Living out God's plan for our lives doesn't mean that we can avoid dealing with our own junk, emotions, experiences, and character. Conversely, there will be times that God allows certain things to eventuate, so that they rise to the surface to be dealt with. Years later, I found it to be an interesting realisation how at the young age of thirteen you can already live a double life. I regularly attended church and acted as the nicest guy around but as soon as I left church, I was someone else completely. The Bible teaches us that nothing good comes from the heart of man, rather "'the human heart is the most deceitful of all things, and desperately wicked'" (Jeremiah 17:9 NLT). Based on my personal experience, the issues of the heart are not determined by becoming a certain age. We all need God's grace to transform us and work in us at every stage of our life.

chapter eight
THE CALL

During my teenage years, I frequently inwardly questioned what the phrase 'call of God' meant. I heard it used in preaching, read it in books, and sometimes even heard it on the radio. I learned with time that the call of God for specific people can be linked to a particular task, time, geographical location, or space, be it an intimate, personal, social and/or public space. For others, the call of God in their lives might be bound to a more general or collective purpose. We don't all have the same call; it is different for everyone.

I am conscious of the fact that the call of God for my life has been discernible. I link it to the book of Ephesians 4:11 NKJV which asserts that, 'He Himself gave some to be apostles, some prophets, some evangelists, and some pastors and teachers....' This verse helped me considerably to understand that I didn't need to search for my gifts because Jesus is the giver of gifts. It also indicated what type of gift I had been given. All I had to do was openly receive, follow, and allow myself to be shaped by His hands to fulfill the call with and through Him. Please understand that this amount of knowledge was not acquired at thirteen years of age nor at twenty years old, but incrementally over time. Usually, the time between the revelation of God's call for your life to the time you accept your calling and put it into practice, a substantial amount of time may have elapsed. Time is necessary for God to shape and mould us, teach us new ways, and reveal new things.

Looking at a particular example in the Bible, we learn that Moses was called from birth to deliver Israel from Egypt. He discovered this calling around the age of forty. However, he was only able to put it into practice another forty years later. I've often wondered if Moses was already too old to fulfill his calling. The answer is quite the contrary — in Gods eyes, it is never too late and we're never too old to accomplish the plans and purposes He has for us. He is the master of the plan. He knows exactly how you are built and what type of abilities and capabilities you have, simply because it was Him who put them all there.

> 'O Lord, you have examined my heart and know everything about me.'
>
> *Psalm 139:1 NLT*
>
> 'And I am certain that God, who began the good work within you, will continue his work until it is finally finished on the day when Christ Jesus returns.'
>
> *Philippians 1:6 NLT*

God knows our strengths and weaknesses even before we know them ourselves. In our life, we embark on a journey of discovery, with God accompanying us. He leads us and guides us through the plans He has set out for us. Psalm 139:16 NLT cites:

> 'You saw me before I was born. Every day of my life was recorded in your book. Every moment was laid out before a single day had passed.'

From the age of thirteen, my dream was to become a professional soccer player, and nothing else. I had been working towards the fulfilment of my dream and I loved every moment of it. I felt invincible on the pitch. I wanted to be seen on TV and earn stacks of money. Being hungry for fame at a young age could be considered good as a catalyst for success or be fuel for negative results. I have a clear memory at this age of the first time God spoke to me regarding my personal calling for service. In this same season of my life, I had just advanced from Sunday school to join our church youth group, and I was about to attend my first ever youth camp. It was great to be amongst all the young people of my church. No more Sunday school, I had been promoted… just kidding.

This first youth camp will forever be branded in my memories, illuminated by the fact that I had reached another important milestone in my life, a term I've designated as the discovery of being called. During a prayer night at the camp, the atmosphere was dynamic and exhilarating. We all sensed the presence of God so strong that barely anyone was standing. Young people all over the place were being touched by the power of the Holy Spirit, speaking in tongues and glorifying Jesus like angels. Centered in the crowd, in a flash I hear a voice inside of me, a voice as clear as crystal. The noise that moments ago encircled me now disappeared. It felt like I was alone in the room accompanied only by the Voice of God. I heard him very, very clearly. His precise words to me were: 'You have been chosen since birth to serve me. I have given you a ministerial gift and a specific purpose in life, that I will reveal unto you at a later stage'.

Instantaneously after receiving that word, the voice was gone and the noises around me flooded back into awareness. Consequently, I found myself crying on the floor without fully comprehending what had just happened. Overwhelmed with feelings of joy, peace, and reverence, I could not contain it. Trying to get up after that experience was impossible as I had no strength even though I was feeling perfectly healthy. I felt no fear, no pain, just pure joy. I looked around me to see that several youth leaders were praying over me as I was stationed on the floor. I had completely lost track of time and I had no idea how long I had been lying there. Eventually one of the leaders came and picked me up. He sat me on a chair and emphasised, 'Don't worry Armando, it's all good. You just had an encounter with God'. There was so much more I wanted to know about what had just happened, but the leader suggested that I'd better get some sleep and that we could discuss it the following day.

As you can imagine, I could not wait for the sun to rise the next day. God had unleashed something inside of me, it was like a raging fire burning within. I got up early, showered and rushed to have breakfast. The main subject of discussion at every table was the same. Everyone was raving about the previous night's experience; how good it had been and how God had tremendously touched everyone. As soon as I saw my leader finish his breakfast, I rushed up to him and asked if we could talk. He was very mindful of my enthusiasm and the urge I had to speak with him about all that had happened, that he simply could not delay this conversation any longer. Frankly, I didn't think I would manage to articulate anything clearly in that moment because I felt like a hand grenade, with the pin pulled out and ready to explode. So, we went into another room, and I told him everything that I had experienced on the previous night. I shared what God had spoken to me, how it had felt, and the impression it had left on me. My youth leader simply looked at me and replied, 'That's great Armando. Well, now you will need to simply continue to grow in your Christian life and God will at the right time reveal unto you more and more of His call'.

I was disappointed because I wanted to hear more about it and at least get some sort of explanation. The leader noticed the obvious disappointment on my face, so he went on to say, 'Armando don't worry too much about it. If God has called you, and I believe He did last night, he will guide you. You are still very young. All you need to do for now is to become a true disciple of Christ. Walk the journey and let Jesus work in you'. After that enlightenment he prayed for me, and we went our separate ways for the day. Momentarily, I felt discontented, but later realised that the leader conducted himself in a wise manner.

The following day we all returned home, and I couldn't wait to tell my parents all about my experience. As soon as Mum opened the entrance door of our flat, I started yelling, 'Mum, God spoke to me. Mum, God spoke to me. It was incredible!' Mum's initial response was to calm me down, then grab my things so she could put them away first before speaking about everything that happened. What a contrast, but you know what? It's a perfect example of what happens in real life sometimes. God reveals something unto you, but it seems that no one around you is interested in hearing it. This was a common recurrence over the subsequent years. I had to learn that we need to wait for the right time before we speak and share what God has put into our hearts. Sometimes sharing it prematurely can be harmful.

Finally, I sat down with mum and gave her every exact detail that I had given the youth leader. I could see tears of joy running down my mum's face, complemented by a big, full smile. 'I have always known that God would call you one day' she acknowledged softly, 'It has been my prayer since I first became a Christian.' She hugged me for a while, and it felt like heaven. The days following were about to get funky. On one hand I still had this type of raging fire inside me, but on the other hand, I started questioning if God had really spoken or if it was just a temporary illusion due to the atmosphere at camp. This fight inside me went on for weeks though I chose not to speak to anyone about it. To my surprise, after a few weeks the fighting went away, and I simply continued my life as usual. What about the word God had spoken to me at the prayer night at youth camp? What about the undoubtable time with God that I had experienced? I learned another valuable and vital lesson which is that if we don't nurture God's call upon our life and decide to follow it with actions, not just with words, the flame will die out and you won't advance in all the amazing and unfathomable things God has called us to. God will reveal to us what He has in store for our lives, but He will never force us to do it. We have freedom of choice just like Adam and Eve had in the Garden of Eden.

I continued attending and being involved in church life, but I was living life my way. This went on from the age of thirteen to eighteen. During those years my life appeared to be normal from the outside looking in. The reality is that I was living a double life. In church I was considered as Mr Nice Guy – the guy who new Scripture and was involved in many aspects of church life, somewhat of an example to the younger kids. Beyond the church walls I was someone else completely, always looking for fights in night clubs and creating trouble everywhere I went with my friends. I relished being at the centre of everything.

I habitually practiced lying through my teeth in every situation, exploiting situations and circumstances to work to my advantage. Keeping pure in my youth as Paul would suggest was non-existent. Contrarily, I had this stinking attitude and arrogance that would make me look very ugly. The worst part of this whole situation was that my parents were oblivious to my double lifestyle for all those years. They only saw me as a great son and follower of Jesus. But was I really? If I'm honest, no I wasn't. I was simply a church attendee. Yes, I had several experiences with God, but I somehow always deliberately chose to go my own way.

I was fully aware that God had called me, not exclusively due to my experience at that camp years earlier, but because God would constantly remind me when I found myself in the darkest moments of my life. I constantly fought this conviction by fabricating excuses and reasons why now was not a good time to pursue the calling God had for me, but rather to follow my own desires. My responses to God sounded like, 'I'm not a good Christian as of yet, wait till I'm better' or, 'Let me finish my apprenticeship first, then I will get to that', and my favourite, 'After I buy a nice car and get married'.

The only constant desire in my life during those years was the desire to become a professional soccer player. I pursued this goal with all my strength and all my soul. I was so close to reaching my dream, when three months before my eighteenth birthday I received news from the soccer club agent. He reported that the same scout that had seen me play was interested in discussing a possible transfer to a second division professional team. This meant that I would get paid and receive sponsorship. When the news broke out at home, Dad was happy, but Mum was unsure. She was justifiably concerned that if I was to become a soccer player, I would forget God and church. Back then this type of argument would really irritate me, even though I knew that Mum didn't mean for anything negative to come from it. This was a major crossroads moment in my life. On one hand, I knew exactly what God had told me throughout all these years. Every day was a constant reminder that my life was supposed to be at His service, outworking His specific purpose for my life. On the other hand, I was so close to reaching my lifelong ambition of becoming a professional soccer player. I wanted to follow this passion and desire. Since a little boy, I would dream about it with eyes open, seeing myself running around in the big stadiums of the world, scoring goals for my team. In my mind, I could even hear the crowds cheer me on. I could feel the atmosphere penetrate through my body as if it was tangible and right in front of me.

For weeks, the club agent was engaged with the scout to discuss details. I was also kept in the loop, but I would not always tell my parents everything. This was a golden opportunity that I could not miss. If I missed this opportunity, was I going to be given another shot? Most probably not. This predicament made me feel so conflicted. My heart was full of joy knowing I had been given this amazing opportunity. Conversely, I felt like Judas Iscariot, the one that betrayed Jesus. I know that is a very strong comparative figure, but that thought constantly replayed in my mind. I knew I had an important choice to make that would determine the trajectory of the rest of my life. I innately understood what the correct decision was for me to make, yet I still refused to follow through with it with firm resolve. I knew God was patiently waiting to hear my choice.

One evening after a training session, my trainer called my name, 'Armando, we have an offer on the table'. With eyes watery and shiny he concluded by saying, 'I know you'll do good. Don't ruin this. You know how many of your fellow players would like to be in your place right now. Let's talk tomorrow'. I took the tram to get home, as I would do routinely after every training session. Although, this time it felt considerably different. I had this overwhelming feeling of being crushed by the unbearable weight of a massive rock. I felt as if I was suffocating. Suddenly, I found myself in the same state as I experienced in my first youth camp. I felt isolated from everything, the only sound I could hear was God's voice. Instantly those horrible, oppressive feelings from just moments ago that were persisting for weeks were now gone. I could finally breathe and think clearly. God started to speak, and it was so clear. It was that unmistakable voice inside of me again, resounding throughout my whole body, mind, and spirit. A voice so gentle and peaceful, not forceful in any way but comparable to a gentle breeze of wind. God explained to me on that tram that I had a choice to make, and that either way He would bless me, and I will receive the desires of my heart. The difference though is that one of those choices God would tolerate, the other choice would be the outliving of His perfect plan. It is exactly here in this moment that I realised God was giving me the opportunity to choose and use my free will. Now that the cloudiness in my mind was gone, I was at long last able to think straight and concentrate on what I wanted for my life, in God and with God.

When I arrived home exhausted, I briefly told my parents about the offer and went to bed. The next morning, I woke up different. I felt light and free. I hadn't felt like this for months. Curiously, the desire to become a professional soccer player had diminished overnight. Meanwhile the desire to serve God Almighty had dramatically increased again in such a powerful way, that it's difficult to correctly illustrate this supernatural feeling. It felt like my eyes were now open and I could see what God sees. I would not have visions of playing soccer in a stadium, but of myself preaching in a stadium. I know that this hasn't happened yet, but one day it will. That same day, I rang my head coach and team agent and refused the offer. I just knew in my heart, that it was the right decision. A decision led by God for my life. For once I desired to do as God had said. For a moment it felt like my life was slipping away from me, yet simultaneously I knew that it was going to be substituted by something bigger and better. To this day, I don't really know how I managed to choose wholeheartedly God's perfect will for my life. I can attest that it has only been possible through the help of the Holy Spirit.

After the phone call to my club, hell broke loose. Everyone was so upset with me. No one was able to understand my decision, the whole team declared me a complete fool. Many negative words were spoken out towards me that day, but I thank God for His protection. It took several weeks for the whole situation to calm down. I was eventually kicked out of the club and another player got presented the offer.

On the 25th of September 1994, the day of my 18th birthday, I informed my parents that I had decided to enrol myself into Bible college after I finished my apprenticeship. I had decided that this was the time to turn my whole life around. I started off by leaving behind all the bad friendships and influencers that were in my life. This also caused a few dramas as you could imagine. Once I had cut off all the negative friendships, I focused on establishing new friendships that would help me grow and change. Now I had time to properly focus on my apprenticeship studies, which I hadn't focused on for so long.

A few months after this dramatic conversion, I decided to take the next step of faith and get water baptised. Lots of my new friends came to support me. My whole family was overwhelmed with joy. I was ready to publicly declare that I was a follower of Jesus. When I think back to this time in my life, I cannot deny God's hand in all of it. I cannot refute all the prayers my mum prayed in my favour. Even when things were dark and hopeless, God's plan continues to advance, even after hitting milestone after milestone. This same still goes for today. God's methods don't change. He remains the same yesterday, today, and forevermore. What we need to understand is that God has a plan for each one of us, which is stipulated way before we are born.

Over the course of our life, God will reveal aspects of His plans for us as He sees fit. Plans that only do us good. All we need to do is trust Him and embrace His plan and purposes for our life. Easier said than done friends. It is possible but there will always be a price to pay. The million-dollar question is are we willing to pay it?

chapter nine
A NEW LIFE

This is where the rubber hit the road and God completely turned my life around. In February 1997 I left Mannheim, Germany, to become a student at the International Bible Training College near London, in a little place called Burgess Hill in Western Sussex. I didn't really know much about the IBTI, other than a few friends and my pastor suggested that I attend, as they had only ever heard good things about it. Little did I know that this was not only going to be a theological learning experience, but so much more than I could ever expect. God used this time to transform me completely. During this time of transition and growth in my life, I was being set apart to be cut and polished. In this place God dug out things deep inside my soul that needed to be taken out. It was also the place where I received fresh teachings that renewed my thinking and approach to life. Maybe you're wondering if this place really exists.

It does, and it still operates today with the same vigour and mission as it did back then. By then, I was changed, ready and anticipant. There was still a small hurdle that I needed to overcome, the English language.

Throughout my school years, even though I attended English class for five years, my proficiency in the English language was just about non-existent. I never paid attention during class and neither did I apply myself to study. Now that I had come so far, and I wanted to learn more about God, how to serve him, and how to be a better disciple. I wouldn't let a new language hinder me from achieving my goal. At that point I already spoke fluent Albanian, Italian, and German. After some contemplation I decided that it couldn't be that hard to learn English. With tenacity I enrolled at an additional English class at the college. Throughout the day I would attend my usual subject classes, then in the evening I would learn English. Surprisingly, learning English wasn't as hard as I had imagined because my brain began to recall countless things that I had learnt during my high school English classes. Right when I thought I had never paid attention to anything, my brain opened a draw where all my knowledge of the English language was stored. I genuinely enjoyed learning a new language, and within literally less than six months, I was fluent and able to write, talk, and lead a conversation. My English wasn't perfect, but it was close. Naturally, my new understanding of the English language made things in my life significantly easier on so many levels. I always disliked studying in my youth, but I learned to love it. Prior to my engagement in my studies at IBTI, I never applied myself to study in any circumstance before, but now it seemed that I couldn't get enough of it. I find it incredible how by the grace of God things change, even those things we think impossible. I couldn't believe that a country boy from a small village of 10,000 people was studying in London.

As the adage goes 'It's not how you start that's important but how well you finish'. In this initial phase of frequenting the IBTI, I learned that it doesn't matter where you have come from or what you have done up until that point. This is simply because God's plan for our life has always existed, even when we walk on the fringes of it. For God, nothing changes and nothing catches Him by surprise. He knows the end from the beginning. I met so many beautiful people at the IBTI, from various places and walks of life, and I thank God that I was able to learn something new from each one of them. Even though it was great being there and it felt like heaven at times, God had to continue His work in me. Of course, I was there to learn and be transformed, but that's easier said than done. This process takes time, effort, and pain.

God started to show me things in my life that needed to be either let go of or changed into good. At first it wasn't easy to accept certain things, let alone to allow God to work on it. One of the first things that happened during that time was the hunger for deeper understanding; to know more about God and seeking the things of above. As it is written in Matthew 6:33 NKJV, '…seek first the kingdom of God and His righteousness, and all these things shall be added to you.'

I never had that type of hunger before, but now it seemed like I wanted to devour every page of my Bible. Studying the Word of God was calming and fulfilling. I observed that my fellow students were stressed, especially during exam time, dissimilar to me as I was relaxed and ready. I understood that in our Christian walk, being hungry for the things of God is vital. The Word of God becomes our new source of nourishment that feeds and satisfies our three dimensional being: Body, Soul, and Spirit. The Word of God strengthens them and makes them strong.

This is also exactly what I experienced during my full forty-day fast. Too many Christians starve to death spiritually because they don't eat properly. They may only read quick verses here and there or a synthesised message on some Bible app. Please don't misunderstand me, I'm not saying this is wrong but simply that it is not sustenance enough for a disciple of Jesus. One of my favourite Bible verses that my mum encouraged me to learn by heart at the age of ten is written in the book of Joshua 1:8 NKJV.

> 'This Book of the Law shall not depart from your mouth, but you shall meditate on it day and night, so that you may be careful to do according to all that is written in it. For then you will make your way prosperous, and then you will have good success.'

This was exactly the lesson God was teaching me in that moment. You see friends, the Bible is not just an optional book that Christians can read when they have nothing else to do. It should be the book we orient ourselves towards to find directions. It is our personal spiritual compass, where we find the indications and instructions we need for life. Through this we discover who God is.

Unfortunately, from the year 2000 onwards, God's Word seems to have lost its significance amongst Christians. The importance of teaching and reading the Bible has lost its strength, therefore sound practice has been lost. That verse in Joshua is very clear, this 'Book of the Law shall not depart from your mouth'. We have so many other words in our mouth, that often there is no space for the Word of God to be in there and present itself when needed. Before I decided to follow God wholeheartedly, this is exactly what happened to me. I heard the Word of God, but I would never keep it 'always on [my] lips' as the NIV translation stipulates. There is a clear message throughout the whole Bible that having God's Word in our heart, hands, and mouth is of unparalleled importance. Having the Word in your mouth and in your heart is the consequence of meditating on it day and night. God was teaching me that reading, studying, and meditating on His Word was never supposed to be just an option, but rather an indispensable daily activity that generates strength, hope, and knowledge.

Sadly, in these days, this principle is not thought about and acted upon as much as it should be. Now, I'm not saying that it will be easy to apply this habit instantly in our lives, but it's achievable with God. If God is encouraging us to do it, then it means that it can be done, otherwise God would not request it. God is good, and because of that He goes the extra mile, promising us that if we mediate on His Word daily, He will reward us. Then we have the promise that we will succeed in all our enterprises. Who doesn't want to succeed in life? God gives us the key for success, but in our ignorance or laziness we keep the key in our pocket as optional. Changing my reading habits from time seldom spent in the Word, to being more intentional and frequent was not easy. There were days where I really had to force myself, and there have been other days where I failed completely. Either way, God always understands. The idea is to always remain as focused and consistent as possible in doing the things we know to do. Whilst God was teaching me to always remain hungry for his words, He was simultaneously extracting things from my life that were toxic, one of them being fear.

I used to be horrified of the dark. In my childhood, I had experienced several demonic activities. There was one specific instance that changed my life forever. I was nine years old, and my little brother Stefano was five years old when we had this encounter. For several days we were sleeping over at my aunt and uncle's house because our parents had to go away for business reasons. Conveniently, their house was right in front of ours. We loved them and had no issue staying with them.

When the first night fell, the horror started. What seemed to be a normal night turned very quickly into a demonic nightmare. As my brother and I snuggled up nicely in our bed, trying to fall asleep, we suddenly felt a demonic presence invade the room. We were petrified because we could sense and feel the atmosphere in the room shift and the temperature drop. We could also hear very heavy breathing noises next to our heads. We knew something was standing right next to us. With no strength to shout or to even move our lips, every single muscle in our bodies were completely stiff due to the immense fear. We simply hugged each other and stayed like that all night. In the meanwhile, the room had become a horse racing parlour. We could hear beasts running around in circles and all sorts of other dreadful noises. Since that night, my life was forever changed. The next day we called our parents and our pastor, explaining to them what took place the previous night. My brother and I were scared to death. The thought of staying in that room again chilled me to my bones. To my surprise, my parents told us that unfortunately we could not go anywhere else, and that if it were to happen again, God would protect us. This rose the spontaneous question, 'Where was He last night? We nearly died!'

The pastor came to see us and tried to comfort us. In case it happened again that night, he gave us further instruction on what to do; we knew we had protection in the blood of Jesus, we had authority in His Name, with wisdom and guidance in the Bible. Still terrorised but full of hope, the second night fell, and we were back in that room. Once the lights were turned off, we prayed, covered ourselves with the blood of Jesus, and had the Bible with us in our bed. For a while, it was calm. I could only hear both of our little hearts racing and pounding aloud as we were hugging each other tightly. It didn't take long before the whole scenario started playing out again. We were scared to death. It's impossible to completely describe what we felt in those two nights. Those supernatural events downright changed my life, and I became horrified of being in the dark. I was not able to enter any dark room and would get heart palpitations just thinking about nightfall. This would happen in any house or any place. I wondered why God didn't protect us, and why the blood of Jesus didn't work after we had specifically prayed for it. I had so many questions and I was angry.

This fear installed itself into my life at the age of nine and stayed there for years until the age of twenty-two. For many years I lived with this secret fear. I prayed and fasted about it, asking God to take it away but it seemed like nothing was happening. During the day I was bold like a lion, but at night I would go into panic mode. I remember that even as I grew older, I still hated the night. I tried my best to keep busy during the dark hours with at least one light on in the room to not fall asleep. The best solution I had for having a peaceful sleep was to keep a light on. This was routine for fourteen years.

One day at IBTI in England, I simply decided to pray about this secret fear, and I honestly sensed something transpire in that moment. It was dusk as I was outside walking around the grounds in prayer, yet I could feel the very strange and real fear rising once again. In a flash I felt something leave my body. I don't know how that happened so instantaneously, but I knew its name was fear. An immediate sense of relief rushed over me, something I had not experienced in a very long time. I was free, Jesus had set me free. The spirit of fear that had tormented me for so long was now gone. It was straightforward, no shouting, no special occasion or prayer involved, the whole experience was quick and gentle.

Even to this day, I remember the feeling of deliverance. I had been delivered from the spirit of fear. I know there are a few theologians out there that will not agree with me, but truthfully, I don't really care because I am confident that my experience was authentic. From that day on I was able to enter dark rooms with no fear and was able to be in places I couldn't before. That overwhelming feeling of fear rising was finally gone from my life forever. I realised how God was watching over me and that He was transforming me, starting His good work from the internal towards the external. Although, the work required in me was not yet finished, much still had to be done.

> 'So all of us who have had that veil removed can see and reflect the glory of the Lord. And the Lord—who is the Spirit—makes us more and more like him as we are changed into his glorious image.'
>
> *2 Corinthians 3:18 NLT*

God is not in a rush. He is not bound by space and time. His plan is determined, and He will follow it through to the very end. God has transformed me completely and I believe He will transform you also if you are willing.

chapter ten
A BROKEN HEART
PART ONE

This will be one of, if not the most remarkable story you will read regarding my life. It's literally movie material. However, please don't focus too much on it. Try to see the lessons in it, which are more valuable than the drama. The only reason why I decided to include this specific event in this book is to testify of the goodness of God, and how He can restore any broken heart.

Whilst in at Bible college, in late 1997, I decided to go back home for the Easter break. Life was great. I was having a fantastic time with all the students, and relished studying my favourite book, the Bible. God was teaching me new things and was continuously working in my life. Everything was picture perfect. Returning home to be with the family for the first break was a wonderful and special time. Over the break, I reconnected with a girl whom I knew from years past. Let's call her Rose, for the sake of the story. Rose was good looking, charming and had sparkly eyes. I fell in love immediately. The moment I saw her I wanted to be with her. It didn't take long for me to express my feelings towards her. To my surprise, she declared her feelings to be mutual. This brought great joy to my heart. It felt so surreal. I kept on thanking God for her. We prayed together and dreamed of the future ahead of us.

My days at home were limited, as I would have to return to college soon as the Easter break was coming to an end. So, we tried to be together as much as possible. In the meanwhile, everyone around me including my family, friends, and pastor raised their concerns on how quick our relationship was developing. 'You are running and not thinking straight', my dad would emphasise. 'Are you sure it's the will of God for your life?' my pastor questioned. Inside, I was so sure of it. I didn't like being asked all these questions. Of course, I had asked God, and I felt as if the answer was 'yes' — it had to be, I was madly in love with Rose. Just because I couldn't think straight, did that mean I couldn't be with her? In hindsight, those weeks spent with her blurred my vision, disabling me to see certain things that I should have picked up on much earlier. I was deaf to the advice of many people around me and closest to me.

Everything was running so fast, and when you run fast your surroundings can become hazy, and you may not be able to see obstacles right in front of you. Therefore, it can turn quickly into a dangerous experience, spinning out of control until you fall hard. The problem when you are so madly in love is that you don't realise or anticipate these things beforehand. The saying 'love makes you blind' was a very real experience for me.

Window shopping in front of a jewellery shop one day, Rose and I stood there dreaming about our future together, as you do when you are young and madly in love. Time appeared to be standing still. 'I have an idea!' I exclaimed in front of the jewellery shop. 'Let me buy you a ring now and get engaged immediately'. What a crazy thing that was to do. Getting engaged is serious business. Did I truly mean that I was fully committed to marrying that girl, and spending the rest of my life with her? Such a decision should never be taken as lightly as I did that day. My excuse was that I was madly in love, therefore it was acceptable to do a crazy, spontaneous thing like that and to let my feelings and enthusiasm take the lead. Overjoyed and watery eyed, Rose looked at me and asked, 'Would you really do that now?' 'Let's go in', I replied. So that day she chose her ring, and I chose mine, as is custom in Italian tradition. We were over the moon. What did we just do? Now it was time to share the news. We each rang our parents to inform them of the news and understandably, they were not happy at all. My parents were furious. 'This is going too far!' Mum yelled over the phone. 'Come home please, let's discuss this.' Rose's parents were a bit cooler about it, but obviously displeased at the situation we all found ourselves in. We decided that for the remainder of the afternoon that it would be best to separate, to go home to our parents and explain our actions.

What you need to understand is that our crazy act goes against all the cultural teaching we were taught since childhood. An engagement, within an Italian family context, is something to be taken very seriously and not to joke about. Honour and pride are so intertwined in our culture that it is disrespectful if taken lightly. Engaging in such a momentous life choice means a great deal to the parents and future parents-in-law. Our foolish action, as you would imagine, had unleashed a problematic series of events. When I eventually got back home, my parents were already waiting for me. When I opened the entrance door, my dad's face was red with anger and my mums face was downcast. The consequences of my irrational act of love had just hit me. I wouldn't have thought that it would cause such turbulence. I should have known better because I was taught these principles all my life and was very familiar with our traditions and customs.

I sat down with my parents and explained that I didn't mean to create such a storm. I certainly didn't mean to disrespect them. I was crazy in love with Rose, and all I wanted was to make her happy and marry her soon. My parents were not against Rose nor against us being together nor even getting married. They were simply concerned that we were rushing this process, without thinking of future consequences. Both of my parents tried to bring God's purpose for my life into the picture. I was reminded of His plan and desires for me and my future wife, plus the fact that I should have sought God's face more to discover His will in this circumstance. They were clearly being good parents, helping me to see the bigger picture in life, but I didn't want a bar of it. I closed myself off and didn't want to listen to reason.

Every so often we do the exact same thing in our Christian walk, we rush through major life decisions without waiting for God's guidance. Other times we are so stubborn that God doesn't get the chance to talk sense into us. Does this sound this familiar to you? Have you found yourself in such situation? Well, it's normal. We have all been there. If we don't give God the place and space to talk to us, He simply will not do it. He will always allow us to have the freedom of choice, but at the same time He will remain with us, He will never leave us nor forsake us. He loves us too much to do anything contrary. He will wait patiently till we are able to listen. Occasionally, we may ask ourselves why God doesn't answer us… well maybe because we are running from what He has already said, or we are not ready or willing to listen to what God has to say. One thing I have learned is that it is never God's fault when we don't get what we want. Delays usually happen as a direct result of our own faults and shortcomings. Remember the Israelites? Forty years in the desert, not because of God, but because of their own exploits. However, God didn't stop helping, caring, and watching over them.

After a long conversation with my parents that day, we agreed that it would be best to get together with the future in-laws to further discuss the best way to handle this sudden engagement. Two days later we all met and agreed to throw a party, inviting family and friends, making our engagement official and public. This would at least keep everyone happy and aware that we were serious about our relationship, and that marriage was on the table. With only four days left before I had to return to England to pursue Bible College, I was overwhelmed with joy, my life was like a dream. Finally, I had found happiness and satisfaction. Rose was fantastic and the future looked bright. Rose and I talked a considerable amount about marriage and how we would tackle this upcoming time of separation. It was a bittersweet moment; we knew that it wasn't going to be easy. I deduced also that I could not put all my focus on this time of separation, rather to focus on my studies so as not to jeopardise this opportunity. I had come so far, I couldn't risk it and I wasn't willing to give it all up. My dad always taught me to finish what you start, so that is what I intended to do. I promised Rose that I would marry her straight after Graduation Day, exactly one and half years from that time. She was insistent on getting married promptly… or at least by the end of my first year in college. She would say, 'our love is strong, we can do it', but I was hesitant. Even though I loved Rose, rushing into marriage this quick was too big of a step that this time I couldn't follow through. After several discussions, she realised that I wasn't going to change my mind about it, and accepted the fact that it would happen in one and a half years' time.

The seventh of January 1998 marked when I flew back to England to finish my studies. I remember this date so well because it was such a melancholic day at the airport. Rose was there, along with my family and friends, all in tears, wishing me goodbye. The hardest part was being separated from my family and Rose. The ugly feeling of separation was killing me that day. It felt like someone was ripping my heart out of my chest. I literally felt a type of physical pain which I had never felt before. I know it sounds a bit dramatic, but I can assure you the feelings were legitimate. Despite the pain, I knew that I had to finish what I had started. I knew what God's call upon my life was, and now I was going to share that same calling with someone else.

Let's pause the story for a moment. I have a question for you? If you're called to serve God with a specific ministry call, does your wife need to be on board as well? Does she need to be called as well? Does this not make it even more difficult to find someone to share life with? A few difficult questions I know, but these are all valuable, precious, and indispensable questions we must ask ourselves. The answers to these questions reveal an abundance of insight regarding how your future will look when you are in such a situation. What do you think? Truth is, that if I had asked myself these questions beforehand, I would have had better foresight. These questions are uncomfortable yet of extreme importance. They can't be ignored because we may fear the answers. This is not a matter to be swept under the carpet, ignoring, and trying to forget the truth as I did. The people around me were asking these questions, but I refused to listen. Truth is, that if we are called for ministry, then both need to be called in ministry. You cannot live life where only one of the two is called, it makes it extremely difficult to do ministry like this. If both are not walking in the same direction, the marriage relationship will eventually break down. People that are not called to ministry are not always able to understand the weight that needs to be carried, sometimes they are also not willing to pay the price for it. This is not to criticise anyone, but we have too many examples around us that confirm this. Unfortunately, it all too often ends up in drama, pain, and suffering — all because no one dared to discover the answers to these vital questions. The solution could have been very simple if I asked myself these very questions at a much earlier stage in the relationship. I am certain that then I would have at least had an inkling of what was to come.

Even if being apart from Rose was hard, the days at Bible College were flying. Several months had passed since I had seen Rose, but the fact that we would soon be together over Christmas was giving me strength to carry on. We would phone each other often and write love letters to each other nearly every day. For my birthday towards the end of September, she called me, and we had great time talking over the phone. It was so good to hear her voice, like music to my ears. We were happy and kept on talking about how amazing it was going to be to finally see each other again soon. After a while, we ended the conversation, and as I put down the phone a strong thought flashed through my mind that something was not right, something wasn't sitting well inside of me. The days, then weeks passed by, and that thought did not return. It seemed strange that right after my birthday, when I last spoke to Rose, she didn't call me as frequently, nor would she send me love letters like she did in the months prior. I didn't think anything bad about it, I just thought she did not have much money left to call, or she was too busy with work.

My first year at the International Bible Training College was coming to a successful end, as I was getting ready to fly out from London on the 23rd of December 1997. I arrived at the airport in Frankfurt am Main, in Germany, and my dad was already waiting for me at the pickup area. My heart bounced because I was so happy to see him. Strangely enough, Rose wasn't there, so I thought that she hadn't received the ok from her employer to take some time off to see me. After hugging my dad, I asked him where Rose was. He looked at me with puppy eyes said, 'I'll tell you all about it in the car'. Well, now I was certain that something was off. I was eager to get to the car so I could hear all about it. However, nothing could have prepared me for what was coming next.

chapter eleven
A BROKEN HEART
PART TWO

Once the suitcases were in the boot, I jumped into the front seat and asked immediately, 'Where is Rose and what is happening?' My dad didn't know where to look, neither did he know how to articulate what he was about to say. He simply said that she was gone. In that moment, my old self rose from the ashes. The old feelings of anger and violence came flooding back. I was out of control in that car, to the point that it was getting dangerous to carry on driving. Only by the grace of God did I manage to calm down after a while. Then my dad proceeded to give me further information on this shocking news. 'Armando', he empathised, 'It's been a few days now since Rose left her parents' home. She left behind a letter explaining that she could not follow through with the engagement, and that she wished to live another life. She also explicitly asked not to search after her, nor did she desire any contact with anyone. In fact, her parents, brothers, and friends had tried to find her but with no success. She simply disappeared and no one knew of her whereabouts. Lastly, she also left the engagement ring on her beauty table, to give it back to you.' Not only was I in shock, I was devastated. My heart had sunk to my stomach, and my soul felt so crushed, that after an attack of anger, I could hardly breathe.

For the remainder of the journey home, I sat in complete silence. There were thousands of thoughts rushing over me like an avalanche, threatening to bury me in my own thoughts. The only question I could formulate in my mind was 'why me, why now?' None of this made any sense. I pondered if this was a joke or if this relationship was fake the whole time. I didn't know how I could have seen this coming.

I was deeply wounded and bleeding, like a deer hit by the arrow of a skilled hunter. It was so abrupt, and now I was left standing to face this adversity. Once I arrived home, my family embraced me, and I cried for a long time. I later asked my parents if we could immediately go as a family to visit Rose's parents, with the intention of trying to understand more about this crazy situation I found myself in. On the way to their house, the all too familiar anger from the past once again invaded my heart. The only thought that entertained my brain at that moment was to punch my now ex future father-in-law right in the face. I was attributing this situation to him. I believed that it was his fault that this happened because he didn't educate his daughter well enough. I know it sounds absurd, but I was convinced it was so.

Once we arrived, I was ready to punch him as soon as the door opened; I knew it would be him opening it as it was his custom. As the door opened, and I was getting ready to swing at him, the unthinkable happened – he jumped towards me, kneeling at my feet, and asking forgiveness. 'Please forgive me Armando', he cried out with tears running downs his cheeks. In that moment, I felt both ashamed and humbled. All of that built up anger and those bad intentions vanished in an instant. I picked him up off the floor and comforted him. I responded to his plead of forgiveness with the words 'that's ok' as we walked somberly inside the house. We stayed with Rose's family and talked for many hours. Everyone tried to make sense of what had happened despite being astonished and dismayed at her unforeseeable choice. They explained to me that everything seemed normal with her at home, and that's why no one had any suspicions that anything like this would happen. The police were even contacted, but considering she was over the age of eighteen and had left voluntarily, there was nothing that they could do.

The next day, I called a few old friends to ask if they could help me find her. To cut a long story short, in less than twenty-four hours I was given the address to where Rose had moved. She was roughly thirty kilometres away in a nearby city. I didn't tell anyone at first that I had the information everyone wanted. I decided that I wanted to face the situation first on my own. This required me to take a train first, then a taxi until I reached the exact address I was given. It was Saturday, the sun was shining but it was very cold. As I arrived at the destination, I entered the courtyard and could immediately hear Rose's voice. She was singing. She loved to sing and would take any opportunity to do so. As I approached her door, her voice became increasingly clear. I was shaking as I reached my arm out to ring the doorbell. I wondered what her reaction would be seeing me standing at her doorstep. I pinched myself, took a deep breath and rang the bell. As she came to the door to open it, our eyes met, but in a flash, she slammed it shut. From the other side of the door, she blurted out, 'What are you doing here and how did you find me?' followed by, 'Go away please'. In the split second that the door was open – I wasn't sure if I had seen right – but she was pregnant. I was in disbelief and shock. Had I seen it right or was I imagining this? Now it was more than just anger brewing from deep within, I was now fuming. As this drama kept unfolding itself, I couldn't help but bombard her with the all-important question, 'Are you pregnant?' I desperately needed to hear the truth. 'Why did you do this to me?' I continued demanding that she open the door before I kicked it in. I still wonder today how not even one of her neighbours called the police on me. 'I just want to talk', I repeated, 'just talk, Rose. Open the door please'. Eventually, in distress she gave in and opened the door. I didn't want to make a bad situation worse, so we found a way to calm ourselves down enough to have a proper conversation. She explained that she had met another man whilst I was studying, and that one thing led to another, and she fell pregnant. She described her shame and her uncertainty of how to approach the predicament she found herself in. Consequently, she thought the best thing for her to do would be to leave me and everything else behind and start a new life.

To the question, 'are you living with him', she replied 'no'. She was obviously lying because I could see his belongings lying around the house. I was trying to remain calm whilst listening to her, but she kept on distorting the truth, which was driving me nuts. I was not only fighting on an emotional level in this situation, but the internal inferno within me was ready to wage war. Eventually, she confessed that after they found out she was pregnant, they decided to keep the baby, move in together, thereby taking me out of the picture completely. She informed me that she was now four months pregnant, and due to her being unable to hide her tummy anymore, she wrote the letter of goodbye and left. This of course, raised a multitude of questions for me like 'how it was possible that no one noticed her growing belly after three months?' I was totally crushed, and my heart was in so much pain that I felt like throwing up. I couldn't look her in the eye, I couldn't bear the fact that the woman I loved had betrayed me like this. No words could adequately express or describe the anguish I felt that day. Several hours had passed, it was around 2.30pm when I heard a car arriving inside the courtyard. I knew simply by looking at Rose's face that it was him, her new man. She cried out and implored me not to hit him. That inferno within took over me and erupted, causing the undesirable events that followed. Rather than going into detail, as this will not help anyone, I will say without reservation that I deeply regret what happened that day. How could I possibly go from the new, transformed version of myself, just to strip myself down to my old ways? I have pondered and wished many times since then that I had not gone to find Rose to seek an explanation from her, it probably would have spared me a lot of pain. Anyhow, as it turned out after all the theatrics, Roses' new man brought me home with his car. Yes, you are reading this correctly, he drove me home. Don't ask how I convinced him.

When I arrived home at my parent's place that evening, I was absolutely destroyed. I cried for hours, and my parents were very concerned about me; they had never heard me cry like this, and at that point in time they didn't know what had eventuated that day. That night I cried myself to sleep, only to wake up the next day like a zombie. Several hours into the morning, I gathered enough courage to tell my parents what had happened. They were also clearly devastated. That day we prayed and cried together deeply, choosing to forgive and forget, and asking God to help us and everyone else involved. The days that followed were a nightmare. We visited Roses' parents to relay the series of events that had transpired. We unanimously decided that it would be best to pause any contact between us whilst we were trying to recover. How could I go back to Bible college after this? Regarding Rose and her new man, we agreed that we would never see each other again. With Roses' parents, we also decided to cut off communication. Christmas had turned out to be a complete disaster that year. Mum was repeatedly encouraging me to go and speak to my pastor in town, but I didn't really have the strength to do so.

Meanwhile, I only had one week left before having to go back to England to start my second year at the IBTI. I felt ashamed and embarrassed. How could I call myself worthy to be a Bible college student when all I saw before me was nothing but unpleasantness? To me, it appeared as if my hopes and dreams for a bright future had been wiped out in one fell swoop. All the joy and satisfaction I experienced before I left for my end of year break was gone, completely non-existent. I was so close to giving up. I wanted to call the college and cancel my enrolment. What future was I going to have now that all my hopes and dreams were totally crushed? It was impossible for me to see anything but negativity at that time. It was as if I was falling into a nasty depression, slowly drifting into a dark place. I strongly believe that the only reason I didn't fall into deep depression was because of the prayers of the saints. After the news broke out about what had happened, and people seeing me in that horrible state, everyone started to pray for me.

I would see my mum pray for me day and night. I could feel the power of prayer uplifting me. Two days before my departure a miracle occurred. As I woke up that morning, all the sorrow was suddenly gone, the emotional pain was lifted. I felt a revival in my soul. I couldn't explain what had happened. It was surely a miracle, I even looked different. So, I decided to return to my studies and let God do what He does best, which is restore people. Believe me folks, the subsequent months were not easy, even after the first miracle of restoration. Now I had to deal with emotions of unforgiveness towards Rose, anger against God, and many other things. I had to deal with this all while studying hard to successfully graduate from college that year.

God is good. He is gracious with endless patience towards us. He understands when things go well and when they develop into a drama like I faced. It took several months to fully recover from a broken heart. Some months later, I was informed that Rose and her partner had lost their baby only a few weeks before the due date. They ended up separating, and unfortunately life only took a turn for the worst for Rose after that. She continued with a lifestyle full of dramatic circumstances and events, worthy of being made into a movie. Be that as it may, it's not up to me to tell her story. The great thing about this though, with thanks to God, is that she has a story of redemption she could tell herself if she wished to do so one day. After the infamous day when we went our separate ways, we did not meet again until many years later, twelve to be precise. I saw Rose back in Church, married and with children. I'm thankful to God for the work He has done in both of our lives, because today we are able to tell of what He has done.

chapter twelve
HEALING & REDEMPTION

After I had recovered from my love drama, I was able to engage with God on what my future should look like. My second year of studying at the IBTI was progressing and I was growing steadily in both my personal and spiritual life. The question, 'What will I do next?' was amplifying in my head. 'Will I ever find the right woman for my life? Will I be able to do ministry alone?' Legitimate questions one may say, and of course they are. Yet I was still too scared to face them even after all I had gone through, I was somewhat sceptical. I also wondered, 'Was God, going to give me the right woman for life? Was I able, to accept her?' Maybe you have gone through something similar or maybe something worse. One thing that I have learned through this ordeal is that God can always redeem someone if he or she is willing. God can always mend a broken heart, like He did for me. Nothing is too hard for Him. When you find yourself in a dark valley it's very difficult to see the light, let alone what lies beyond. Remember that the calm always follows the storm, no matter how tempestuous. The Bible mentions a fantastic promise made to us in 1 Corinthians 10:13 MSG.

> 'No test or temptation that comes your way is beyond the course of what others have had to face. All you need to remember is that God will never let you down; he'll never let you be pushed past your limit; he'll always be there to help you come through it.'

Understanding this truth is of great worth because in times of trouble it gives us hope, strength, comfort, and peace. It gives us the assurance that God will not allow for us to be destroyed. What a great promise to help us endure times of testings and tribulations.

Dear friends, hardships are needed in our life because they help us to grow. I know it's painful, but it's beneficial to us. Hardship teaches us new things, it allows us to receive new revelations from God, and purifies us from stubborn and toxic thoughts, habits, and strongholds in our life. The testing of our faith can be compared with the process of purifying gold. Through a process of very high temperature heating, the impurities from the gold rise to the surface to then be skimmed off by the goldsmith. Spiritually speaking, God is our goldsmith. He is the one who leads the process. He reveals the impurities from within our hearts and sanctifies us. He brings about our real beauty. Through this refinement we are led to repentance, which allows us to reflect the beauty of our Saviour Jesus more accurately. He is also the one who protects the gold during the process of refinement. In my case, I went through the fire, but I didn't burn.

Several months later at Bible college, I decided to do a short, full fast – meaning no food at all, only water. During this fast, the intention was to ask God to secure my future and to help me see what he sees. As well as that, I asked that He provide a wife in my near future so that we could both serve Him together with a ministry. I was well-aware that I had received a call to ministry. Under no circumstances did I want to jeopardise this vocation by marrying the wrong woman. I quickly realised early in the fast that my perspective on this delicate subject had changed. Before the fast, I had been a bit looser as to who you could marry as a Christian – look at where this led me.

The reality is, if I stopped for just a moment to think and listen to all the questions and concerns that my family and friends had, I believe all that drama would have been avoided. The important point here is that we need to seek God's will in everything we do, well before we engage in anything.

If we engage in something, and we are uncertain that it is Gods will for us, then it is practically too late. You see, when we want to serve God for real, we can't play supermarket. What do I mean by that? A simple explanation is when customers go to the supermarket to purchase a product. If they are not satisfied with the product, all they need to do is simply return it for a refund or exchange, but life doesn't work like this. This is especially true as a Christian seeking a love relationship. You cannot simply go out into the world to buy and try, and then exchange or get a refund if you are not satisfied. Christians must act according to the will of God first. If you have God's green light, then you engage. I learned that the hard way; once I fell in love with Rose, I went for it. However, when it came to knowing if Rose was Gods' will for my life, it constantly felt as if I was backpedalling. Truth be told, I never received a confirmation from God that she was the one for me. I tried to convince myself that God was ok with it because I loved her. I refused to listen to the advice given to me due to the fear of losing her. There was no way I was going to make the same mistake twice.

During that time of fasting, I asked God to orchestrate everything Himself. In fact, I expressed to God, 'If there is to ever be a girl that you bring before me, please know that I will not move one finger in trying to win her. I will not attempt to create any romantic atmosphere, nor will I engage in anything of the sort. You, God will need to make it all happen'. My mind was set and unwilling to make any compromises, too scared that I would mess it up. Only a short time later did I discover that God was ok with it, and that He was about to do exactly what I had asked for.

At some point during the night at the end of my fast, I had a God-given dream. It was a dream that gave me hope and filled me with peace. I dreamed of a woman dressed in a wedding gown. She was of petite stature, and well-proportioned with an excellent physique. I couldn't see her face as it was covered by a champagne-coloured veil, although her long and curly dark blonde hair was very visible. I recall that in my dream I was astonished by her beauty. I was looking at her intently, trying so see more of her face but I couldn't. As I was standing there trying to get a closer look at this woman's face, I hear a voice that says, 'Get ready, this will be your future wife'. The next morning, I woke up a bit shaken. I wondered if I really had a God-given dream that revealed to me my future wife, or if it was due to my overactive imagination since I had spoken so much about it in the last few days. In my confusion, I inquired of God if this dream was authentically from Him, and God answered yes. For some reason, I felt incapable to accept that it was for real, and that God had indeed given me a glimpse into my future.

In that moment, I learned that when we go through some very tough times in life, it's nearly inevitable that these experiences leave behind some sort of residue in us. A residue, that if we don't deal with it and decide to give it to God, will slowly influence our belief system. In other words, it will hinder us from believing for something new. I understood that I had to give these residues to God, otherwise it would ruin my belief system.

Even though I wanted to believe that this dream was from God, the doubts crept in, and I found myself unable to hope and fully believe in its authenticity. God had to help me in the following weeks to give Him the things that were negatively influencing my belief system. Remember how Jesus responded to Martha in John 11:40 NLT, "'Didn't I tell you that you would see God's glory if you believe?'" The same principle applies to us today; if we don't believe we will not see His glory, nor the things we have hoped for. We need to keep our belief systems intact, otherwise we will miss out on what God want to give us, do in us, and through us.

After my belief system was reset, I started to hope again and learned to be joyful about the future. I knew God was holding me close. I kept on trying to remember how that girl in my dream looked like, but with no success. The weeks and months passed, and the dream slowly faded away. My final year at IBTI marked the fiftieth anniversary of the college, and a large celebration was planned. You can just imagine all the preparations required for such an event; students on a mission ran around everywhere, and there were people arriving from all over the world to join in on the momentous celebrations. Most of the guests were former students that had left the IBTI many years earlier and had gone on to fulfill their God-given calling in their lives.

It was a very busy time for me. I was studying for the final exams and helping to organise the historic occasion, all while continuing to learn and grow spiritually, hoping to receive the answers to my prayers. The day of celebration had finally arrived. You'd expect the workload would diminish at least temporarily with all that was going on, but it was quite the opposite. It was imperative that the students attended to the guests, therefore the workload increased.

In the course of my time at college, I befriended a fantastic lady named Carmelina. She was Italian like me, and extremely kind, bubbly, and overall loving. Everyone in college loved Carmelina. In fact, some friends of mine and myself included called her "Apostle Carmelina". We gave her this nickname because we were convinced that she had all the attributes to become an apostle.

On the opening day of the college's 50th anniversary, Carmelina was particularly excited. Her senior pastor and a group of young ladies from church were coming from Belgium to celebrate together with her. In fact, her senior pastor was a previous student at the college, so you can imagine Carmelina's joy. Over the course of the day, Carmelina introduced me to Pastor Baudouin Galanty and the group of girls that had come with him. Admittedly, I probably came across as cold and arrogant initially, due to my decision of not wanting to move in any direction unless I had the green light from God.

A few days went by and nothing overly special happened. As a student, I carried on with my daily tasks and looking after the guests. One thing that was added to my task list throughout the celebrations was to play the role of English to Italian translator. It was my responsibility to simultaneously translate the services that were held during the morning and evening. I love translating, it's something I have always enjoyed. Little did I know that something unexpected was about to happen to me one morning on duty. On this specific morning, I was running late. I forgot my Italian Bible in my room, so I missed out on receiving the full rundown of the service and where my position was going to be within the service tent. After I retrieved my Italian Bible and arrived at the tent, I rushed to find the student in charge of handling my translating equipment. As I'm looking around the room, suddenly but very clearly, I hear God's voice announcing, 'Turn around now and you will see your future wife'. In that moment I didn't know what to think, but by pure instinct I followed orders and made a sharp, quick turn behind me, totalling maybe two seconds. I was bewildered as I turned around because approximately two metres away one of the Belgium girls was standing right there. I didn't even know her name. In that moment what struck me was her golden blonde, long curly hair. I also noticed that she was taken by surprise because I turned around so abruptly.

After I turned back around, I knew what God had just told me but somehow, my brain was slow to respond.

Quickly enough, I had the revelation that I had already seen that hair, and in an instant my eyes were opened, and I remembered the dream I had months earlier. I couldn't believe what had just happened. Stunned, I thought to myself, 'What do I do next? I must stay calm, simply say nothing, and perform my duties'. So that's exactly what I did, I pretended like nothing happened, though you could imagine how I was feeling after that brief experience, with ten thousand thoughts rushing through my mind. For the remainder of the day, I repetitively asked God, 'Is it really her? Did I really hear from you?' He replied every time with a resounding 'YES!' I promised myself that I will not take any initiative towards girls anymore, which is exactly what I did. I didn't approach her, speak to her, or attempt to explain why I had abruptly turned my head towards her. Instead, I incessantly prayed, asking God if it really was her, the woman in my dream, my future wife. If it was, He would have to create a special moment where we could officially meet and get to know each other. This would have to happen fast because Carmelina's pastor and the visiting group of ladies were heading back home to Belgium in four days.

'God, you make it happen if it is your will', I restated. It was nearly the weekend, and Carmelina came to see me, asking if I was interested in joining her and the Belgium group the next day to go to the beach. How do you think I replied? With an assertive yes of course. My heart was just about pounding out of my chest, and full of joy. Carmelina simply replied, 'That's great, I will add you to the list so that we can arrange the cars accordingly'. I was over the moon because the answer I was waiting for had arrived, at least so I thought. I had faithfully kept my promise, I hadn't moved a finger in making any of this happen, so I thought that this must be it. I couldn't wait for the day to end and the next to begin. I remember going to bed that night with mixed emotions, I didn't want to relive the past and get hurt again. I recall praying the Lord's prayer, specifically the phrase 'Your will be done here on earth'. This is forever engraved on my heart.

I woke up to the warmth and light of the beautiful sun the next morning. I was buzzing from the excitement that was planned out for the day. I had to convince myself to calm down. After breakfast, Carmelina approached me with a sad face and immediately I knew that something was wrong. She explained to me that there had been a miscalculation and that unfortunately there was not enough seats available in the cars to take everyone to the beach. She was very apologetic about the fact that I was not able to go, and boy did I feel terrible and angry in that moment. I managed not to show too much disappointment or to allow anything negative to transpire in front of Carmelina.

I went back to my room devastated. I grabbed my pillow and put my face in it and started screaming like a mad man. It took a while until I lifted my head up from that pillow. Once again, I felt deeply betrayed somehow. I was angry with myself for believing this could be a reality, and I was also angry at the devil, attributing to him this deceitful manoeuvre. Truth be told the devil had nothing to do with it, and I hadn't done anything wrong in believing again, although I didn't realise it in that moment. I stayed in my room for many hours that morning, which was a rare occurrence, but that morning was different. After lunch I decided to go and play ping pong with the other students to take my mind off what happened that morning. In the middle of a match, my good friend Riccardo randomly asked, 'Armando, I'm thinking of going to the beach later, do you want to come?' Without thinking twice, I accepted his offer and asked for some time to freshen up and change my clothes. Riccardo had a car, the only usual passenger being his wife, Veronica.

What I didn't know at that time was that God was using him to bring forth His plan for me. When I was ready, I left to meet up with Riccardo and Veronica. As I walked towards their car, I noticed that one of the Belgium girls was standing next to Riccardo's car. It was her, my supposed future wife, the one from my dream. Completely stunned, I approached the car to say hello and I asked for her name. 'Isabella — what a beautiful name', I responded.

After we greeted, she asked why I was there. I explained that I was going to the beach with Riccardo. She replied that he had also asked her earlier if she wanted to join, and since she also wasn't able to go with her friends from Belgium due to lack of space in the designated cars, she agreed to go with them. 'Well, the same thing happened to me', I answered. 'But I'm glad I'm here now'. Riccardo and Veronica eventually arrived at their car, we all hopped in and drove in the direction of Brighton beach. With the warmth of the sun on our skin, no clouds, just a clear sky, it was the perfect day to go to the beach. In the car we started talking and getting to know each other more. The atmosphere in that car was something special and memorable. I believe it was a God atmosphere, it felt so good. The more I talked to Isabella, the more I knew that what God had said was true. A sense of unexplainable peace and reassurance overwhelmed me. Once we reached Brighton, determining where to go from there, Isabella and I found ourselves alone. Riccardo and Veronica were gone. I'm not too sure how that had happened, maybe because they noticed a spark between us thus deciding to leave us alone, but I'm uncertain if that was the actual reason. I never dared to ask Riccardo why they left us alone that day, however I'm certainly grateful they did. Once we realised that we were alone, and that Isabella felt comfortable with it, we began walking and talking on the Brighton pier. Time stood still. Love was in the air. She looked exactly like she did in the dream, with her long curly hair, petite and shapely figure. It seemed too good to be true. She was stunning and so sweet. I thought to myself, 'What a gentle soul, so pure and innocent'. I loved every word she spoke. We talked about life, God, ministry, our dreams and considerably more – not necessarily topics you would normally converse with someone that you just met – but with us, it was different. There was a divine symphony between us that I can't explain, a match made in heaven. The hours passed and evening came. We managed to join the Belgium group at a restaurant to have dinner together before it was time to make our way back to the college. Carmelina immediately noticed the chemistry between Isabella and me. She looked intently at me and said, 'You be careful, she is my friend'. I replied, 'Of course, don't you worry'. We all enjoyed our time together that evening, there was lots of conversation and laughter. Back at the IBTI, we wished each other a good night, and went back to our rooms.

As I'm lying in my bed, I'm trying to elaborate in my mind what had happened throughout the day. My heart and mind were full, I could evidently see that Isabella had enjoyed being with me, which gave me lots of confidence and peace. I had several signs reaffirming that she was the one. Naturally, I still wanted more confirmations from God. Since I couldn't sleep that night, I decided to bombard heaven with questions until 5:00am, the main one being, 'Is it really her, God?' At one point, I heard the Holy Spirit saying: 'Stop it now, we have already told you, it's her. Sleep and be in peace. On the other side, she is asking the same thing.' I obeyed, put my head on the pillow, and slept until the alarm clock sounded two hours later at 7.00am. It was Monday morning, and our student life would carry on as usual. I was able to briefly speak with Isabella at breakfast, telling her that I had enjoyed our time together, and then I had to go to class. In my heart, I knew I wanted to be with her and spend time with her. On the other hand, I had promised myself to never rush into a relationship again. Isabella had only two days left at the college before the Belgium group would have to head back home. The day went by in a flash. I didn't attempt to talk to her or try to create any romantic situation, I remained neutral but observant. On the last day, Isabella came and asked if we could write to each other. Without hesitation I replied, 'Of course,

I'd love too. After we exchanged our addresses, we hugged each other goodbye. I suggested, 'Let's be friends, we'll write to each other every week, it will be fun.' Not long after, they all got in their respective buses and left the IBTI. I can still picture Isabella looking at me and waving. That was a sad moment, but I still remember and cherish it. As she left my view, I knew that I at least had the assurance and hope that God had chosen her for my life, and I was chosen for her life.

It didn't take long before I found myself writing the first letter to Isabella. I wanted to be the one to initiate a conversation. I was missing her but didn't want to tell her. So, in every letter that I wrote, my tone was always neutral. I was trying to portray myself as just a friend and didn't want to express my true feelings towards her. I didn't write letters telling her of the things that happened when she was visiting at the IBTI. Neither did I articulate how I felt when I was with her, they were simply friendly and encouraging.

Graduation day was not too far away, and at this point all the students were studying extra hard to pass the final exams. I was so close to the finish line that there was no way I was going to allow anything to mess this up. I was studying every day, trying to understand and learn as much as I could. I wanted to be ready for my exams, but not only ready, I wanted to excel. For once in my life, I wanted to make my parents proud of my hard work and dedication to my studies. I wanted to succeed where I had never succeeded before, and not been seen as a loser. When the final exams rolled around, I passed them with flying colours. I was ecstatic because I had never passed a single exam prior to these ones. Now I was graduating from college with fantastic results. I was so proud of this achievement, and I thank God for all His help along this journey. I couldn't wait to tell Isabella, and I couldn't wait to tell my family and friends. In fact, I couldn't wait to tell the whole world.

After graduation, not much was going on at the college. Everyone was preparing to go back to their own homes, and so was I because I missed my family considerably in the two years I was away studying in England. Especially after all the dramas that went on before I left, my family became an even more important part of my life. I don't know what I would have done if they weren't there for me during that dark period of my life.

I know you're probably wondering what happened between Isabella and me. We continued writing to each other for months yet didn't declare any love or deep emotions to one another. I decided once again to ask God for a sign, an ultimate proof that she was really the one. I asked God three things before leaving Bible college so I would know for certain if Isabella was really destined to be my future wife. God would have to fulfil my last three requests, and only then would I declare my love to Isabella and fill her in on everything. The first request was that before I touched German soil, I would touch Belgium ground first. I know it's a strange request, but that's what I asked. I had no reason to go to Belgium first, since I was heading home to Germany. However, I asked God to change that, and I would see it as a sign that He has once again confirmed Isabella's purpose in my life. The second request was for Isabella's and Carmelina's pastor to ring me and invite me to preach at their church before arriving home. The third and final request was that by some miracle, I would be hosted in Belgium. More than that, to be hosted at Isabella's parents' house. This was a very big deal, since it touches on important values in the Italian culture.

Even though Isabella and I were friends, and had written letters to each other for many months, I was a nobody to her parents. In fact, I was a stranger, and they would have no reason to host me at their home. No one would do that in the Italian culture in a similar situation, especially when no declarations were made, nor any feelings shown. For something like this to occur, a miracle was needed due to the difficulty of these three requests I had made. I knew that if God intervened and brought these things to fruition, I would have no doubts left. Would you believe that only a few days later I received a phone call from Isabella and Carmelina's pastor, Baudouin, asking me to travel directly to Belgium from England. He wanted me to preach at their church before returning home. What an incredible feeling it was when two out of three requests were answered in less than 48 hours. God was on my case. It felt out of this world watching this unfold before my eyes. This meant that I was finally able to declare my love to Isabella and hear from her if she felt the same. However, there was still one more request that needed to be realised, and it was the most difficult one yet. My deepest hope was that God would set the seal on this last petition by performing this third miracle.

In contact with pastor Baudouin, we agreed that he would find me an appropriate place to stay whilst I was visiting Belgium. He mentioned that there was a certain family in the church that were happy to extend their hospitality towards overseas church guests. My accommodation was now secure. Pastor Baudouin also mentioned that the hostess was going first to pick up Carmelina straight from the Bible College as she had too much luggage with her to be able to fly. I was to fly out two days later to allow the ladies time to settle in comfortably.

I arrived on the day and time agreed on previously, and I was trying to reach Pastor Baudouin to let him know, but for whatever reason I couldn't reach him, all the phone calls went straight to his message bank. I called Isabella to let her know that I was waiting at the train station and that pastor Baudouin was not answering his phone. In no time she was at the airport and ready to bring me to her parents' house whilst we were waiting for Pastor Baudouin to reply. It felt a bit awkward being at her place without even having met her parents beforehand. It was a strange situation, but what else were we to do? We sat at the table together enjoying coffee, tea, and cake, then the anticipated phone call came. Pastor Baudouin sounded worried. He explained that the lady who was supposed to host me was having problems with her new car as they were driving from England to Belgium. He explained how he thought it was very strange that something like this would happen to a brand-new car. The car was at the mechanics, and they were trying to fix it as promptly as possible. He resumed by saying that if everything went well, by evening she could be back home with her family. Then they'd be ready to receive me into their home.

It was only late morning when we received this update, so Isabella's mum invited me to stay for lunch saying that I was more than welcome. I had nowhere else to go while I was waiting, so I accepted the lunch invite. This minor setback gave me the opportunity to get to know Isabella's parents, and for them to get to know me. The fact is that it may have seemed like a strange situation, yet God was turning this around to fulfil this last request of mine. In fact, later that day around four in the afternoon, we received another phone call from the pastor, informing us that the mechanics were not able to repair the car on that day. He was going to make few more phone calls to see if he could find another family to host me for the night. The situation was becoming increasingly awkward, but I must say that Isabella's parents took it with class. They kept on assuring me that it was OK for me to be there considering the situation, so we kept on talking and having fun. Isabella's parents kept on asking questions about my life, my plans, and dreams. I must admit, it wasn't a very pleasant conversation. Regardless of that, I realised that her parents were very good people; humble, loving, and of good heart.

Time was flying, but there was still no news from Pastor Baudouin. The phone was silent for a long time. I kept looking at the clock as it was nearing dinner time. The last thing I wanted was to feel like I was imposing, and for them to feel pressured to ask me to to stay for dinner. Before I could even finish that thought, Isabella's mum faced me and stated,

'Since you have liked my food during lunch, I'm sure you will also enjoy the food during dinner. You are more than welcome to stay here and have dinner with us.' At this point, I didn't really know what to think or say, I just kept on nodding in agreement and appreciation. Despite the sticky situation, I was enjoying being with Isabella immensely and being able to simply talk about anything and everything. Getting to know her in her own environment was a blessing. Her demeanour remained as true as when I first met her. This was a good sign, it meant that she was real and authentic.

I couldn't stop looking at the clock. I noticed how time was flying, concerned that Baudouin had still not called and that there was still not solution after so many hours. Could I not simply be put in a hotel for the night? As my mind was racing, I was trying to maintain my cool in this peculiar predicament. I was simultaneously praying that God would finalise this last miracle so that I could reveal my true feelings to Isabella. How I wanted to tell her that I loved her. I wanted to tell her everything that had been going on in the background since we met until this moment; all about God's revelation of her to me, the incredible dream I had before meeting her, and my petition for God to fulfil three very specific requests for a confirmation of these truths. It was as if I had arrived at the end of a complex puzzle, and I was holding the last puzzle piece in between my fingers, yearning to connect the last piece into the puzzle to create the finished picture.

Finally, at 9:30pm the phone rang. Tired, Baudouin explained that the car was still at the mechanics and that he had been trying all day to find me alternative accommodation but with no success. At this point he didn't know what to do anymore. He said, the best thing to do would be to find a hotel room for the night. Just as he was finishing the sentence, Isabella's dad intervened to say, 'No hotel needed, Armando can stay here for tonight and sleep on the sofa bed'. The unthinkable had just happened. The miracle that I was waiting for occurred in front of my eyes. It was incredible, and I was speechless to see how God had manoeuvred throughout the whole day to bring everything to this point. Obviously, I agreed and thanked them for their incredibly generous hospitality. Baudouin was obviously relieved as well and promised that we would find a solution the following day.

The green light was on, I had received all three of the confirmations I had asked God for. I thought about what to do next because at that point, it was already very late. I worked up the courage to ask Isabella's parents if I could stay behind with Isabella to talk to her about something very important. To my surprise, her parents had no objection to that. Once they went to bed, I was able to tell Isabella my story from start to finish. She was able to tell me her story too, which brought joy, peace, and a few tears that evening. We were now finally free to declare our love for each other and we thanked God for all the amazing things that He had done so far. We couldn't believe our story so far; it was like a chapter was taken straight out of a book. We now had one another, and we were both over the moon.

The following morning, we boldly decided to inform her parents about our recent declaration of love. Again, they had no objections. It was a positively great and emotive day. If you're asking if I had kept my parents in the loop, I can reassure you that I certainly did. I had asked them to pray and to support me in this adventure. They were well-aware of the whole journey, and they knew I didn't want to make the same mistake as before and involve them only after the fact. They supported and encouraged me a great deal. I don't know what I would have done without them. I thank them today for all the love and all the patience they had with me throughout my teenage years and beyond. I am still here now thanks to them.

The next few days with Isabella were simply magic. Our love grew to new heights. Our first kiss and holding hands for the first time was breath-taking. It felt so good, my heart was finally healed. I had received full redemption from all negative things in my past. I learned that God is always faithful no matter what. He guided me, allowing me to reach milestone after milestone even in uncertainty, and I believe God will do the same thing for you.

chapter thirteen
THE INVISIBLE CHAPTER

Dear reader, I hope that you have enjoyed reading my story. My heart's desire has always been that this book would not just simply be a good story, but a tool that would reach and help people.

Maybe you can relate to my story, maybe you have gone through something similar. As you read this book, you may have learned some lessons along the way. They could have been easy to learn, or maybe some others were much more difficult. Regardless, I want to encourage you to always seek the will of God for your life. I can tell you with no shadow of a doubt, that following God's plan for your life is the best thing that you can possibly do. It is only when we don't follow God's plan, that we live an unfulfilled life. Only when we do follow His plan, will we find purpose in everything we do.

Rest assured my dear reader, that when we seek

God's Kingdom first, God is faithful to give to us all the things that we need. He has done it for me, He has done it for countless others, and He will do it for you also. My sincere prayer for you is that God will reveal the marvellous plan He has for you. I also pray that you will find fulfilment and purpose in life. I know that life is not always easy, even when we follow God. Nonetheless, we must continue to 'Fight the good fight of the faith'. The Second Man in us will always try to create trouble. He'll always try to gain the upper hand, but if you and I remain faithful and work on strengthening our Spiritual Man, he will have no other option than to bow and let Jesus be King in our lives.

I would love to pray this prayer with you right now where you are. If you feel comfortable doing that, simply repeat this prayer with me.

Dear Jesus, I thank you for the life that you have given me. I thank you for the purposes and plans that You have designed for me before I was even born. Help me Father, help me Jesus, guide me Holy Spirit to discover your ways and the plans that you have for me. Help me to strengthen my spiritual man, so that I can fight off the second man within me. Be the King of my life Jesus, and let Your will be done here on earth, as it is in heaven.

AMEN.

Now you're probably wondering what happened in our lives after the times depicted in this book. Rest assured, my intention has always been to share with you how God blessed my life, and our lives together after declaring our love for one other.

One year later, I asked Isabella to marry me, and we officialised our engagement. Shortly after, in April 2000 we were married, and what an amazing day it was. We desired to have children; our first-born baby girl Leah, was born in August 2001. Our second blessing, Luana-Vittoria was born five years later, through another miracle received from God. After we got married, we decided to do life in Belgium. For that reason, I moved from Germany and went to live in Belgium, in the city where Isabella was born and raised. We stayed in Belgium for twelve years where together we served the Lord. We were part of the same church that she was saved in, and the pastor was our dear friend Baudouin Galanty. I served alongside Baudouin for many years, being on the elder's panel. I would preach, teach, evangelise, and do anything else that was required. After those twelve years in Belgium, God called us as a family to move and reside in Australia, where we've had the privilege to serve in ministry for many years. God's plan had completely unfolded. Now looking in hindsight, I can see how all the sacrifices, all the pain, and all the tears had finally brought forth its fruit. God changed my whole life around. As I mentioned earlier, when God has a plan, He will see it to completion. Trust God in everything, and you will never lack and never be disappointed.

REFERENCES

Preface

So whether you eat or drink or whatever you do,
do it all for the glory of God.
1 Corinthians 10:31 NIV

Chapter One

When they had finished eating, Jesus said to Simon Peter, "Simon son of John, do you love me more than these?" "Yes, Lord," he said, "you know that I love you." Jesus said, "Feed my lambs."
Again Jesus said, "Simon son of John, do you love me?" He answered, "Yes, Lord, you know that I love you." Jesus said, "Take care of my sheep."'
The third time he said to him, "Simon son of John, do you love me? "Peter was hurt because Jesus

asked him the third time, "Do you love me?" He said, "Lord, you know all things; you know that I love you." Jesus said, "Feed my sheep".
John 21:15-17 NIV

When you follow the desires of your sinful nature, the results are very clear: sexual immorality, impurity, lustful pleasures, idolatry, sorcery, hostility, quarrelling, jealousy, outbursts of anger, selfish ambition, dissension, division, envy, drunkenness, wild parties, and other sins like these. Let me tell you again, as I have before, that anyone living that sort of life will not inherit the Kingdom of God.
Galatians 5:19-21 NLT

As the Scriptures say, "People are like grass; their beauty is like a flower in the field. The grass withers and the flower fades.
1 Peter 1:24 NLT

A voice says, "Cry out."
And I said, "What shall I cry?"
"All people are like grass, and all their faithfulness is like the flowers of the field.
The grass withers and the flowers fall, because the

breath of the LORD blows on them.
Surely the people are grass.
The grass withers and the flowers fall, but the word of our God endures forever."
Isaiah 40:6-8 NIV

Therefore, if anyone is in Christ, the new creation has come: The old has gone, the new is here!
2 Corinthians 5:17 NIV

But to all who believed him and accepted him, he gave the right to become children of God. They are reborn—not with a physical birth resulting from human passion or plan, but a birth that comes from God.
John 1:12-13 NLT

Do not lie to one another, since you have put off the old man with his deeds, and have put on the new man who is renewed in knowledge according to the image of Him who created him….
Colossians 3:9-10 NKJV

...and that you put on the new man which was created according to God, in true righteousness and holiness.
Ephesians 4:24 NKJV

"He must become greater; I must become less"
John 3:30 NIV

But store up for yourselves treasures in heaven, where neither moth nor rust destroys, and where thieves do not break in or steal; for where your treasure is, there your heart will be also.
Matthew 6:20-21 NASB

And what more shall I say? For time will fail me if I tell of Gideon, Barak, Samson, Jephthah, of David and Samuel and the prophets, who by faith conquered kingdoms, performed acts of righteousness, obtained promises, shut the mouths of lions, quenched the power of fire, escaped the edge of the sword, from weakness were made strong, became mighty in war, put foreign armies to flight.
Hebrews 11:32-34 NASB

Jesus answered and said to them, "Those who are well have no need of a physician, but those who are sick".
Luke 5:31 NKJV

Chapter 2

For you created my inmost being; you knit me together in my mother's womb. I praise you because I am fearfully and wonderfully made; your works are wonderful, I know that full well. My frame was not hidden from you when I was made in the secret place, when I was woven together in the depths of the earth. Your eyes saw my unformed body; all the days ordained for me were written in your book before one of them came to be.
Psalm 139:13-16 NIV

"Before I formed you in the womb I knew you, before you were born, I set you apart; I appointed you as a prophet to the nations"
Jeremiah 1:5 NIV

"For I know the plans I have for you," declares the LORD, "plans to prosper you and not to harm you, plans to give you hope and a future".
Jeremiah 29:11 NIV

Keep your lives free from the love of money and be content with what you have, because God has said, "Never will I leave you; never will I forsake you."
Hebrews 13:5 NIV

No one will be able to stand against you all the days of your life. As I was with Moses, so I will be with you; I will never leave you nor forsake you.
Joshua 1:5 NIV

Be strong and courageous. Do not be afraid or terrified because of them, for the Lord your God goes with you; he will never leave you nor forsake you.
Deuteronomy 31:6 NIV

I know what it is to be in need, and I know what it is to have plenty. I have learned the secret of being content in any and every situation, whether well fed or hungry, whether living in plenty or in want. I can do all this through him who gives me strength.
Philippians 4:12-13 NIV

A person's steps are directed by the Lord. How then can anyone understand their own way?
Proverbs 20:24 NIV

In their hearts humans plan their course,
but the Lord establishes their steps.
Proverbs 16:9 NIV

Chapter 3

Trust in the Lord with all your heart,
And lean not on your own understanding;
In all your ways acknowledge Him,
And He shall direct your paths.
Proverbs 3:5-6 NKJV

Chapter 4

So Christ himself gave the apostles, the prophets, the evangelists, the pastors and teachers, to equip his people for works of service, so that the body of Christ may be built up until we all reach unity in the faith and in the knowledge of the Son of God and become mature, attaining to the whole measure of the fullness of Christ.
Ephesians 4:11-13 NIV

The Cost of Following Jesus

As they were walking along the road, a man said to him, "I will follow you wherever you go." Jesus replied, "Foxes have dens and birds have nests, but the Son of Man has no place to lay his head." He said to another man, "Follow me." But he replied, "Lord, first let me go and bury my father." Jesus said to him, "Let the dead bury their own dead, but you go and proclaim the kingdom of God." Still another said, "I will follow you, Lord; but first let me go back and say goodbye to my family." Jesus replied, "No one who puts a hand to the plow and looks back is fit for service in the kingdom of God."
Luke 9:57-62 NIV

Many are the plans in a person's heart, but it is the LORD's purpose that prevails.
Proverbs 19:21 NIV

So God created human beings in his own image. In the image of God, he created them; male and female he created them.
Genesis 1:27 NIV

Chapter 5

My old self has been crucified with Christ. It is no longer I who live, but Christ lives in me. So I live in this earthly body by trusting in the Son of God, who loved me and gave himself for me.
Galatians 2:20 NLT

For the desires of the flesh are against the Spirit, and the desires of the Spirit are against the flesh, for these are opposed to each other, to keep you from doing the things you want to do.
Galatians 5:17 ESV

He must become greater and greater, and I must become less and less.
John 3:30 NLT

For we know that our old self was crucified with him so that the body ruled by sin might be done away with, that we should no longer be slaves to sin—because anyone who has died has been set free from sin.
Romans 6:6 NIV

God created man in His own image, in the image of God he created him; male and female he created them.
Genesis 1:27 ESV

God saw all that he had made, and it was very good.
Genesis 1:31 NIV

And they heard the sound of the Lord God walking in the garden in the cool of the day, and Adam and his wife hid themselves from the presence of the Lord God among the trees of the garden.

Then the Lord God called to Adam and said to him, "Where are you?"
So he said, "I heard Your voice in the garden, and I was afraid because I was naked; and I hid myself."
Genesis 3:8-10 NKJV

And Adam lived one hundred and thirty years, and begot a son in his own likeness, after his image, and named him Seth.
Genesis 5:3 NIV

Therefore, just as sin entered the world through one man, and death through sin, and in this way death came to all people, because all sinned—
Romans 5:12 NIV

You disowned the Holy and Righteous One and asked that a murderer be released to you'.
Acts 3:14 NIV

God made him who had no sin to be sin for us, so that in him we might become the righteousness of God.
2 Corinthians 5:21 NIV

For you know that it was not with perishable things such as silver or gold that you were redeemed from the empty way of life handed down to you from your ancestors, but with the precious blood of Christ, a lamb without blemish or defect.
1 Peter 1:18-19 NIV

...throw off your old sinful nature and your former way of life, which is corrupted by lust and deception. Instead, let the Spirit renew your thoughts and attitudes. Put on your new nature, created to be like God—truly righteous and holy.
Ephesians 4:22-24 NLT

Put on your new nature, and be renewed as you learn to know your Creator and become like him.
Colossians 3:10 NLT

For all who are led by the Spirit of God are sons of God.
Romans 8:14 ESV

...in all these things we are more than conquerors through him who loved us.

Romans 8:37 ESV

I can do all things through Christ, who strengthens me.
Philippians 4:13 NKJV

Chapter 6

You made all the delicate, inner parts of my body and knit me together in my mother's womb. Thank you for making me so wonderfully complex! Your workmanship is marvellous — how well I know it.
Psalm 139:13-14 NLT

Don't you realize that your body is the temple of the Holy Spirit, who lives in you and was given to you by God? You do not belong to yourself, for God bought you with a high price. So you must honour God with your body.
1 Corinthians 6:19-20 NLT

How precious also are Your thoughts to me, O God! How great is the sum of them!
Psalm 139:17 NKJV

Then the LORD God formed the man from the dust of the ground. He breathed the breath of life into the man's nostrils, and the man became a living person.
Genesis 2:7 NLT

The Spirit himself testifies with our spirit that we are God's children.
Romans 8:16 NIV

Yes, remember your Creator now while you are young, before the silver cord of life snaps and the golden bowl is broken. Don't wait until the water jar is smashed at the spring and the pulley is broken at the well. For then the dust will return to the earth, and the spirit will return to God who gave it.
Ecclesiastes 12:6-7 NLT

Jesus replied: "Love the Lord your God with all your heart and with all your soul and with all your mind"
Matthew 22:37 NIV

The thief comes only to steal and kill and destroy; I have come that they may have life, and have it to the full.
John 10:10 NIV

Then Jesus was led up by the Spirit into the wilderness to be tempted by the devil. And when He had fasted forty days and forty nights, afterward He was hungry. Now when the tempter came to Him, he said, "If You are the Son of God, command that these stones become bread."
But He answered and said, "It is written, 'Man shall not live by bread alone, but by every word that proceeds from the mouth of God.'" (NKJV)
Then the devil took him to the holy city, Jerusalem, to the highest point of the Temple, and said, "If you are the Son of God, jump off! For the Scriptures say, 'He will order his angels to protect you. And they will hold you up with their hands, so you won't even hurt your foot on a stone.'
Jesus responded, "The Scriptures also say, 'You must not test the Lord your God.'"
Next the devil took him to the peak of a very high mountain and showed him all the kingdoms of the world and their glory. "I will give it all to you," he said, "if you will kneel down and worship me."
"Get out of here, Satan," Jesus told him "For the Scriptures say, 'You must worship the Lord your God and serve only him.'" Then the devil went away, and

angels came and took care of Jesus. (NLT)
Matthew 4:1-11

He humbled you, causing you to hunger and then feeding you with manna, which neither you nor your ancestors had known, to teach you that man does not live on bread alone but on every word that comes from the mouth of the Lord.
Deuteronomy 8:3 NIV

'…for everyone born of God overcomes the world. This is the victory that has overcome the world, even our faith. Who is it that overcomes the world? Only the one who believes that Jesus is the Son of God.'
1 John 5:4-5 NIV

Fight the good fight of the faith. Take hold of the eternal life to which you were called when you made your good confession in the presence of many witnesses.
1 Timothy 6:12 NIV

Chapter 7

'The steps of a man are established by the LORD, when he delights in his way; though he falls, he shall not be cast headlong, for the LORD upholds his hand.'
Psalm 37:23-24 ESV

"The human heart is the most deceitful of all things, and desperately wicked. Who really knows how bad it is?
Jeremiah 17:9 NLT

And we know that God causes everything to work together for the good of those who love God and are called according to his purpose for them.
Romans 8:28 NLT

Chapter 8

He Himself gave some to be apostles, some prophets, some evangelists, and some pastors and teachers....
Ephesians 4:11

O Lord, you have examined my heart and know everything about me.
Psalm 139:1 NLT

You saw me before I was born. Every day of my life was recorded in your book. Every moment was laid out before a single day had passed.
Psalm 139:16 NLT

And I am certain that God, who began the good work within you, will continue his work until it is finally finished on the day when Christ Jesus returns.
Philippians 1:6 NLT

Chapter 9

But seek first the kingdom of God and His righteousness, and all these things shall be added to you.
Matthew 6:33 NKJV

This Book of the Law shall not depart from your mouth, but you shall meditate on it day and night, so that you may be careful to do according to all

that is written in it. For then you will make your way prosperous, and then you will have good success.
Joshua 1:8 NKJV

'So all of us who have had that veil removed can see and reflect the glory of the Lord. And the Lord—who is the Spirit—makes us more and more like him as we are changed into his glorious image.'
2 Corinthians 3:18 NLT

Chapter 12

'No test or temptation that comes your way is beyond the course of what others have had to face. All you need to remember is that God will never let you down; he'll never let you be pushed past your limit; he'll always be there to help you come through it.'
1 Corinthians 10:13 MSG

Jesus responded, "Didn't I tell you that you would see God's glory if you believe?"
John 11:40 NLT